NEW LONDON ARCHITECTURE

KENNETH POWELL

NEW LONDON ARCHITECTURE
REVISED AND EXPANDED EDITION

MERRELL
LONDON · NEW YORK

Published by Merrell Publishers Limited

Head office:
81 Southwark Street
London SE1 0HX

New York office:
49 West 24th Street, 8th Floor
New York, NY 10010

www.merrellpublishers.com

Publisher Hugh Merrell

Editorial Director Julian Honer

US Director Joan Brookbank

Sales and Marketing Manager Kim Cope

Sales and Marketing Executive Emily Sanders

Managing Editor Anthea Snow

Editor Sam Wythe

Design Manager Nicola Bailey

Junior Designer Paul Shinn

Production Manager Michelle Draycott

Production Controller Sadie Butler

First published 2001
Paperback edition first published 2003; revised 2005

British Library Cataloguing-in-Publication Data:
Powell, Kenneth, 1947–
New London architecture
1.Architecture, Modern – 20th century 2.Buildings – England –
London 3.London (England) – Buildings, structures, etc.
I.Title
720.9'421'09049

ISBN 1 85894 310 8

Designed by Maggi Smith
Edited by Mary Ore and Sarah Kane
Proof-read by Kim Richardson
Indexed by Hilary Bird

Printed and bound in China

ACKNOWLEDGEMENTS

In the few years since the publication of the first edition of this book, the tide of big Lottery schemes has dried up and one or two that were in the pipeline – Daniel Libeskind's 'Spiral' for the Victoria and Albert Museum, for instance – have been abandoned. Even so, selecting some key projects for this revised edition was not an easy task, given the dynamism of London and the increasingly enlightened approach of public bodies in the fields of housing, education and healthcare as well as the continued vitality of the commercial development scene. When the first edition was published, Norman Foster's Swiss Re was unfinished: now it is acclaimed as an iconic London landmark. The greatest disappointment is the loss of impetus, under a government that once appeared to be committed to the cause of public transport, of such vital infrastructural projects as Crossrail and Thameslink, while the new Channel Tunnel rail terminal at St Pancras, which ought to be a national showpiece, is a lacklustre addition to Barlow's wonderful shed of the 1860s. It remains to be seen whether the failings of London's transport system will prejudice the capital's chances of succeeding in its bid for the 2012 Olympics.

Kenneth Powell
London, 2005

Front cover and spine: View of the City of London skyline, showing the Swiss Re Headquarters (pp. 232–33); front cover insets (left to right): Mossbourne Community Academy (pp. 138–39), Millennium Bridge (pp. 37–38), BedZed (pp. 154–55), Brick Leaf House (pp. 156–57), Laban Dance Centre (pp. 92–93); City Hall (pp. 206–07), British Airways London Eye (pp. 82–83)
Back cover: Swiss Re Headquarters (pp. 232–33); back cover insets (left to right): Royal Opera House (pp. 108–09), Media Centre, Lord's Cricket Ground (pp. 96–97), Wellcome Wing, the Science Museum (pp. 76–77), Wellcome Trust Headquarters (pp. 236–37), Cookson Smith House (pp. 158–59)
Frontispiece: Great Eastern Hotel (pp. 84–85)
Page 2: Hammersmith Health Centre (pp. 128–29)

CONTENTS

The view from Tower 42 across London: a commercial metropolis in constant change, with the Thames as its central artery.

London is a world city where architecture can rarely be discussed without politics, to some degree, intruding. Unlike Paris, Rome, Madrid or Berlin, London has been a commercial, trading city for much of its history. Most of the other leading business cities of Europe – Frankfurt and Milan, for example – are not capitals. London's character bears the memories of a court-versus-commerce tension that extends back five hundred years; hence the two cities of London and Westminster and the lack of grand piazzas, processional avenues and monumental regal architecture. London is not only a political and commercial capital, it is also, by European standards at least, still a metropolis, with a large population and strong industrial roots. Its economy is equivalent to that of smaller member states of the European Union. Heathrow Airport generates more wealth than entire provincial cities. Yet London has, until recently, lacked a city government: the prostitution of its County Hall to a mix of commercial uses (including an aquarium) bewilders foreigners. County Hall's successor, the City Hall at London Bridge City (see pp. 206–07), is an impressive and innovative structure, yet it is effectively a spin-off from an office development.

London's confident, even expansive, mood in the early years of the twenty-first century – it may yet be punctured by recession – comes after several decades of self-doubt and despondency. "Is London dying?" asked the *Evening Standard* in August 1991: "filthy, clogged and dangerous streets" and a population "increasingly homeless, unemployed and desperate" reflected its crisis. There was a good deal of journalistic hyperbole in all this, but Londoners were genuinely beginning to feel that their city was not what it once was – hadn't the Underground once been the envy of the world? Infrastructural and architectural issues figured prominently in London's fight-back. In 1992, during the run-up to a general election in which the Labour Party's hopes were to be dashed, Richard Rogers, not yet a Labour peer, and Labour's shadow arts minister Mark Fisher published

A New London, a blueprint for the renaissance of the capital as "a metropolis of social and ecological harmony" with "beautiful buildings, tree-lined avenues and new parks, where the commonest sounds are voices, footsteps and the buzz of the electric tram …".[1]

In the summer of the same year, the Architecture Foundation, a body that Richard Rogers chaired (and had been instrumental in founding), organized an exhibition called *City Changes* at the Royal Exchange, at the heart of the City of London, that documented the City's recent architectural achievements.[2] In 1986 the deregulation of share trading, a key Thatcherite move alongside the abolition of exchange controls and a pro-enterprise tax regime, had ushered in the 'Big Bang', a huge expansion in financial services. London's global role in this area was given a dramatic boost, and banks, British and foreign, needed buildings capable of housing the new dealing spaces in which electronic trading in currencies and shares could be conducted. By 1992 a recession was biting hard, yet it was reckoned that, by the end of the following year, half of all the office space in the City would have been rebuilt as a consequence of the Big Bang. Office construction from 1989 to 1990, the height of the Thatcher boom, had equalled the total for the previous decade. The *City Changes* exhibition was intended as a celebration of the success of the City authorities in accommodating big new office developments such as those at Broadgate/Bishopsgate (330,000 square metres of offices over and around the rebuilt Liverpool Street station) and Ludgate – another 'over the tracks' scheme totalling 76,000 square metres – while caring for the City's four-hundred-plus listed buildings and twenty-two conservation areas. Both Broadgate and Ludgate were promoted by Rosehaugh Stanhope, an alliance between developers Stuart Lipton and Godfrey Bradman that set the pace for the renewal of London's commercial building stock. Lipton and Bradman had studied the 'fast-track' construction methods that prevailed in the United States and they proceeded to apply them to solving London's increasingly desperate shortage of new-style office space. At Broadgate (where the first four phases were designed by London-based Arup Associates) and at Ludgate, Skidmore, Owings & Merrill, the most prominent of a series of American architectural practices that had opened London offices, applied skills learned in Manhattan and Chicago. The use of prefabricated parts and the application of novel construction management methods were key elements in a revolutionary (by British standards) approach to design and construction. The more leisurely approach pursued at Richard Rogers's Lloyd's of London – which took eight years (1978–86) to design and build – now seemed irrelevant, while the exquisite and painstaking reconstruction of Bracken House (the former *Financial Times* building) by Michael Hopkins & Partners was clearly a one-off, a matter of biting the bullet handed to the Japanese developer when the building was unexpectedly listed.

The City's reconstruction campaign, which focused on the replacement of supposedly obsolete post-war office buildings (which nobody loved), had, in fact, been only a partial success. Against the odds, triumphing over abysmally poor communications and the inherent conservatism of the financial sector, 'Docklands' – a term applied to a huge swathe of riverside between Tower Bridge and the Thames Barrier – had managed to invade the traditional preserves of the 'Square Mile'. Canary Wharf had originally been conceived by American developer G. Ware Travelstead, who commissioned Skidmore, Owings & Merrill to draw up a 1985 masterplan for a huge new office city on the site of the redundant West India Docks. From 1987 onwards, Travelstead's successor, Olympia & York (which had developed New York's World Financial Center), realized the vision, capitalizing on the financial and planning incentives offered by the London Docklands Development Corporation (established in 1981 to regenerate the abandoned docks). With architecture predominantly by Americans (Skidmore, Owings & Merrill, Kohn Pedersen Fox and Cesar Pelli, who was responsible for the landmark, stainless steel-clad 1 Canada Square tower), Canary Wharf was hard hit by the recession of the 1990s, but by the end of the century was a huge commercial success, with up to 60,000 office workers based there and two new 93,000-square-metre towers flanking Pelli's 1980s icon, one of them designed by Pelli, the other by Foster and Partners.

For some critics, Canary Wharf epitomized the failings of Thatcher's London – "a symbol of 1980s smash-and-grab culture" was the verdict of Samantha Hardingham in her

Above
The Broadgate development spearheaded the redevelopment of the City in the later 1980s.

Opposite
Richard Rogers's Lloyd's of London, completed in 1986, remains one of London's most striking modern monuments.

sharply focused guide to London architecture.[3] Rogers and Fisher, surprisingly, praised its "solid and serious attention to urban design". The neatly maintained private spaces of Canary Wharf and Broadgate contrasted with the unkempt mess of the South Bank. Here was an area of London where the civic and commercial, idealistic and pragmatic, aspirations had confronted each other. It was here that they might profitably be reconciled, yet the history of the area was depressing. After the closure of the Festival of Britain, the Tory government had torn down everything on the festival site save for the Royal Festival Hall. (Ironically, the site for the festival had been created by demolishing streets of terraced houses that had survived wartime bombs.) The area between Waterloo station and Blackfriars Bridge fell into limbo. Richard Rogers's Coin Street project was subjected to planning inquiries in 1979 and 1981 and finally abandoned in the face of opposition from the Greater London Council. (The GLC, facing abolition by the Tory government, ceded its land holdings to a local community group, which began to build social housing there.) The GLC had been responsible for a major new cultural development on the South Bank in the 1960s, but when the Council was abolished, responsibility for this passed to a nominated board. Subsequent attempts (by Stuart Lipton, with Terry

Farrell, responsible for a previous scheme for the site commissioned by the South Bank Board, as architect) to use a degree of commercial development to fund upgrading of the declining South Bank arts centre foundered, while Richard Rogers's 'glass wave' for the South Bank, generated by a 1994 competition, was also widely opposed as an attempt to enclose and privatize public space. By the end of the century, a new masterplan by Rick Mather was in place, with a series of competitions proceeding for the design of individual components in the planned reconstruction. Meanwhile, Coin Street Community Builders, which had incurred critical censure for its unimaginative approach to new housing, changed its tune and commissioned schemes from Lifschutz Davidson and then Haworth Tompkins. But the debate over the South Bank continued – should it be developed to serve London, the world city, or maintained as an amenity for the small local population? The negative attitude of community activists in the area reflected an indifference to the needs of London as a whole.

The 1980s development boom produced much that was mediocre, characterless and transparently designed with a fast buck in mind. Yet it was also a period when a new generation of property developers came to the fore with a taste for distinctive architecture. They included Geoffrey

The first phase of development at Canary Wharf was masterplanned and designed in the United States.

Terry Farrell's Embankment Place was one of the prime landmarks of the commercial Postmodernist style.

Wilson and Stuart Lipton, who had been Richard Rogers's clients for the abortive Coin Street project on the South Bank. Wilson commissioned Terry Farrell to design the massive Embankment Place scheme above Charing Cross station and was later part of the consortium that planned the abortive Classical Revival redevelopment of Paternoster Square. Lipton seemed omnipresent. Even as Broadgate got under way in the City, he was starting work on Stockley Park, the most celebrated of the new out-of-town business parks that appealed particularly to the new technology-based industries and to research-and-development operations. The Stockley site was a former rubbish dump close to Heathrow airport and the M4 motorway, on the wealth-generating corridor out of London to the west. Arup Associates were responsible for the masterplan for the site, with buildings commissioned from Norman Foster, Skidmore, Owings & Merrill, Ian Ritchie, Troughton McAslan and others and set in lavish landscaping. Stockley Park became a showpiece of new British architecture and was also a huge commercial success, underlining Lipton's conviction that good architecture represented a sound investment. In the 1960s developers had established relationships with 'safe' commercial practitioners and stuck with them. The 1980s saw developers launching high-profile design competitions

for prominent sites – Paternoster Square, Bracken House and Stag Place, for example. Stag Place addressed the future of a site close to Victoria station, where a 1960s block owned by Land Securities was to be replaced. There were submissions from the cream of the London architectural scene, including Terry Farrell, Arup Associates, Ahrends, Burton & Koralek, and Richard Rogers, but the winner was Richard Horden. Horden, ironically, was later dropped. (A revised version of his scheme by the EPR practice was later built and is currently occupied by the Office of the Deputy Prime Minister.) Horden's entry for another major competition staged by Land Securities, for Grand Buildings on Trafalgar Square, was also critically acclaimed, but was unplaced – Horden did not achieve the success that many had predicted for him.

Back in 1964, when Ian Nairn pronounced London "one of the best cities in the world for modern architecture", a development boom comparable to that of the 1980s was well under way: London had its first tall buildings, including the Millbank Tower, New Zealand House, the Hilton and the Shell Centre, and the post-war dominance of the public sector was rapidly ebbing in the face of the Macmillan boom.[4] The comprehensive redevelopment of areas such as the Elephant & Castle, Notting Hill Gate and central Croydon was led by the private sector, with the planners colluding, as it seemed to critics of the process, in the destruction of London's physical and social fabric. Unashamedly 'commercial' architectural practices, such as those of Richard Seifert, Fitzroy Robinson and Gollins Melvin Ward, led the transformation of the City and West End. Seifert's most prominent work, the NatWest Tower (now Tower 42), was completed as late as 1979, to less than universal acclaim. Modern architecture seemed to have sold out to high finance. The anti-development, pro-conservation, pro-community mood that had derailed Rogers's Coin Street had been fuelled by the energy crisis of the 1970s. The identity of London was seen as under threat from developers and their architects. In 1984 the Prince of Wales's crusade for a more "humane" architecture was launched; singled out for particular condemnation were Ahrends Burton & Koralek's National Gallery project ("a monstrous carbuncle") and Peter Palumbo's Mansion House Square ("a glass stump", originally designed by the late Mies van der Rohe). The style wars of the 1980s were under way. It was a war between two visions of London. The prince saw the aspects of London that he admired – Georgian terraces, City churches, green parks and squares – as the reflection of an orderly tradition of urban management inspired by a limited monarchy. Yet Wren and Nash were radicals in their day, as Richard Rogers pointed out. The prince seemed to have no comprehension of the real achievements of the Modern Movement or of the fervour for change that inspired the young architects of the Festival of Britain, Golden Lane and the Churchill Gardens estate and made them despise the stultified neo-Georgian of Sir Herbert Baker and Sir Reginald Blomfield.

The prince triumphed at the National Gallery (Ahrends Burton & Koralek fired, Robert Venturi subsequently hired) and at Mansion House Square (the Mies tower dropped), and his taste underlay the choice of Sidell Gibson for the redevelopment of Grand Buildings on Trafalgar Square – "an attempt to create a building no one would notice", commented the *Architects' Journal.* At Canary Wharf he appeared to have succeeded in getting the height of the Pelli tower reduced – the architect later complained that the proportions had been spoiled – but the real culprit was the Civil Aviation Authority, concerned with the safety of approach routes to the new City Airport. The prince's influence gave an (unintentional) boost to the rise of Postmodernism, a manner rapidly taken up by the leading commercial practitioners such as Fitzroy Robinson, Chapman Taylor and Building Design Partnership (BDP),

but responsible for a string of genuinely memorable buildings by James Stirling, Terry Farrell, Piers Gough, Jeremy Dixon and John Outram. Stirling, widely acclaimed as the greatest British architect of the post-war era, finished only one building in London during his lifetime, the Clore Gallery extension to Tate Gallery (now Tate Britain), completed in 1985 and a work remarkable both for its subtle contextualism and for its dynamic internal spaces. (Of the many unbuilt schemes by Stirling submitted for major London sites during the 1980s, the most remarkable was that for the National Gallery, a forceful response to history and place). For Charles Jencks, the Clore was one of the "canonic" Postmodern buildings of London, of which the real pioneer was Jeremy Dixon's St Mark's Road housing of 1976–79. For Jencks, writing in 1991 (as the London development machine ran out of steam), Postmodernism was "the modernisation of Modernism", a way towards a modern architecture both practical and popular. "Post Modern London means a diverse and contradictory city", Jencks wrote.[5] Postmodernism, Jencks argued, had effectively forged a new "London School" of architecture. Certainly, whatever its absurdities, it fuelled a new pluralism and, it might be argued, a willingness to countenance alternatives to the Modernism that had ruled unchallenged since 1945 and produced much that was grim and, to use a favourite adjective of the Prince of Wales, inhuman. Though turned into a tedious parody of itself in the wrong hands, Postmodernism possibly opened the way to an acceptance of an expressive new modern architecture of form and colour during the 1990s and finally buried the myth of functionalism. It was no accident, for example, that Andreas Papadakis of *Architectural Design*, for a decade or so the most influential opinion-former on the London scene (he published the first monographs on Richard Rogers, Quinlan Terry and Will Alsop), moved on from promoting Postmodernism to launching deconstructivist architecture in Britain. (For the old moderns of the RIBA establishment, the two were equally suspect – deviations from the true gospel – and London was slow to recognize innovative talents generated by its own schools.)

The literal classicism that the prince championed had few takers among developers, despite the success, in a suburban context, of Quinlan Terry's Richmond Riverside. While able to secure the abandonment of schemes by Arup Associates and Richard Rogers for Paternoster Square, an area of obsolescent 1960s offices north of St Paul's Cathedral, the prince saw his own favoured project for the

The Clore Gallery at Tate Britain on Millbank was the only building in London completed by James Stirling in his lifetime.

Norman Foster's Sackler Galleries at the Royal Academy, completed in 1991, were hailed as a masterly fusion of old and new.

area, launched by classicist John Simpson, shelved; a low-voltage, but basically modern, masterplan by William Whitfield was subsequently adopted. At Spitalfields, on the eastern edge of the City, classically inspired development proposals by Quinlan Terry and Leon Krier fell flat, while John Simpson's Venetian-style pastiche at London Bridge City was equally still-born. (A design competition for the latter development had produced an outrageously camp Gothic proposal by Philip Johnson, a shameless paraphrase of the Palace of Westminster.) A pompous neo-Georgian masterplan for rebuilding the government office quarter at Marsham Street was jettisoned under New Labour.

Some of these schemes were victims not of changing tastes but of economic realities. The 1990s recession saw sites at London Bridge City II, Spitalfields, the King's Cross goods yard (where Norman Foster had won a 1987 masterplanning competition), the Paddington Basin, Battersea Power Station, Paternoster Square and the South Bank all shelved, pending better times. "The party's over", commented the *Architects' Journal*. Canary Wharf developer Olympia & York was forced to call in the receivers. Among City schemes placed on ice were those by Richard Rogers for Daiwa on Wood Street and by Norman Foster for a site close by on London Wall, though Foster – who had built little in London – completed his Sackler Galleries at the Royal Academy in 1991, setting a benchmark for 'new–old' juxtapositions.

The (temporary, as it turned out) demise of Olympia & York in 1992 was sparked by the company's inability to make an agreed payment of £40,000,000 towards the construction of London Underground's Jubilee line extension, which was seen as the catalyst that would finally release Canary Wharf's real potential. The following year, however, John Major's government gave the go-ahead to this monumental project, completed seven years later. With Roland Paoletti as impresario, the project renewed the idea (generated by Charles Holden and Frank Pick between the wars) of the Underground as a patron of progressive architecture. With contributions by Michael Hopkins, Ian Ritchie, Troughton McAslan, Chris Wilkinson and Norman Foster, the Jubilee line extension looked set to be a showcase of the dominant High-tech tradition, soon to re-emerge on the commercial scene. But commissions to Richard MacCormac, a refined Postmodernist, van Heyningen & Haward and Will Alsop, a genuine original who belonged in no established school of design, underlined Paoletti's determination to produce buildings that responded to the variety of London itself and to eschew the uniform

aesthetic approach favoured by Pick. The Jubilee line extension, completed behind schedule and over budget, nonetheless emerged as the most important exercise in architectural patronage in London since the Festival of Britain.

In spite of itself, it seemed, the Conservative government backed significant investments in London's infrastructure – Nicholas Grimshaw's Waterloo International Terminal was completed in 1993, though there was to be a long wait for the first Eurostar. New road links and the extension of the Docklands Light Railway improved the prospects for Docklands and opened the way for the development of the Royal Docks, the largest and most remote of the dock complexes (and the last to close). Margaret Thatcher's campaign against the welfare state had a huge impact on the housing, health and education sectors, but by the mid-1990s practices such as Avanti Architects and Penoyre & Prasad were producing distinguished social service architecture in the tradition of Lubetkin, Lasdun and Edward Cullinan, while new approaches to housing, pioneered, for example, by Dickon Robinson at the Peabody Trust, began to fill the gap left by the decline of the public rented sector. "While London drifts, Paris has tackled its problems with enterprise, even daring", argued Rogers and Fisher.[6] Paris had its *grands projets,* yet London's equivalents were to come, the product of the National Lottery that the Major government launched in 1994. The perception that London had suffered from the policies of the Tory years was, however, widespread. The abolition of the GLC, which even Thatcher's great inspiration, Enoch Powell, had argued against, was seen as a vindictive and counter-productive move – the need for Londonwide co-ordination of transport and other infrastructure was argued by the City and by business interests. Unlike other Britons, Londoners generally backed higher spending on public transport and further restrictions on private car use – the Tories' transport policies helped to lose them many seats around London, though New Labour was slow to begin remedying the critical problem of movement in the city and south-east region.

Towards the end of New Labour's first term, in fact, the government was locked in a destructive confrontation with London mayor Ken Livingstone over the future funding of the Underground that was resolved only after some very hard bargaining. Thameslink 2000, providing a frequent mainline rail service between north and south London and parts beyond, looked set to go ahead, with three major new stations, and the long-awaited east–west CrossRail link

Nicholas Grimshaw's International Terminal at Waterloo station, completed in 1993, was a pioneering landmark of the new railway age, built to handle Channel Tunnel trains.

finally got the green light (though it will take ten years to build). A decision seemed imminent on plans for a fifth terminal at Heathrow Airport, a project won in competition by Richard Rogers Partnership in 1989 – the scheme, the subject of a record-length planning inquiry, had been strongly opposed by west London communities, but was widely seen as inevitable (and which, indeed, is now under construction). As much could not be said of the high-speed Channel Tunnel Rail Link, planned to carve its way through Kent and terminate, inexplicably, at King's Cross – with marginal gains for travellers content to use the more central terminal at Waterloo. Yet the project won determined backing from the government, intent on reviving the regeneration agenda for the King's Cross area contained in Foster's abandoned project for the goods yard.

When London surfaced from recession in the mid-1990s much of the baggage of the recent past had vanished. The Prince of Wales's influence had decisively waned – his decision to rename his Institute of Architecture to the Prince's Foundation and move it (in 2000) from Regent's Park to a converted warehouse in Shoreditch was symptomatic of new thinking in princely circles. The

Classical Revival was back where it started, in the world of country houses and estate villages – though Quinlan Terry quietly got on with a substantial commercial development in Baker Street. Traditionalist architecture was left to wealthy enthusiasts such as Christopher Moran (who brought in architects Carden & Godfrey and a team of experienced craftsmen to create a convincing neo-Tudor mansion around Crosby Hall, an extraordinary medieval survival removed in the 1890s from the City to Chelsea) and director Sam Wanamaker who, against all the odds, built the new Globe Theatre with Theo Crosby as his architect. Even HM The Queen employed Michael Hopkins for the visitor centre at Buckingham Palace. Nobody would own up to being a Postmodernist. The POMO fashion evaporated even more quickly than it had arrived and many commercial practitioners dropped the sub-Stirling manner in favour of sub-Foster. Its legacy has yet to be dispassionately evaluated. If one project sums up the reforming urban ambitions of the Postmodernists it is Dixon.Jones's Royal Opera House (see pp. 108–09), first conceived by Jeremy Dixon in the mid-1980s as a collage of contrasting elements, breaking down a cultural megastructure into what appears to be a random accretion of city buildings. While the Royal Opera House was being completed, however, its architects had moved on to a cooler and more rational approach, boldly expressed in their extension to the National Portrait Gallery (see pp. 66–67). Stirling Wilford's Number 1 Poultry could be glibly dismissed as an instant period piece, especially since it was completed after James Stirling's premature death in 1992, but commands respect as an ingenious marriage of public and commercial space with genuine civic feeling. Meanwhile, Piers Gough of CZWG continued to build with wit – what other architect has as his best-known work a public convenience? – but failed to win the large public commissions to which he aspired, possibly because nobody would take him seriously. Richard

MacCormac moved on from an over-preoccupation with detail, reflected in some of his Oxbridge college schemes, to the noble spaces of Southwark station (see pp. 44–45) and the dramatic simplicity of the Wellcome Wing at the Science Museum (see pp. 76–77), though his masterly project for Spitalfields was consigned to the bin. William Whitfield, a practitioner of an older generation whose confident 1960s additions to the late Victorian Institute of Chartered Accountants building in the City had been lavishly praised by Nikolaus Pevsner, was seen as the only architect capable of welding together Modernist and traditional elements to make an acceptable masterplan for the long-disputed Paternoster Square site (see pp. 228–29) – Whitfield's Richmond House in Whitehall, with a façade

Stirling Wilford's Number 1 Poultry was the outcome of a twenty-year campaign by Peter Palumbo to develop the site at the heart of the City.

in a sort of streamlined Tudor Gothic style, is one of the oddest London buildings of the post-war era.

Without doubt the most idiosyncratic major London building of the 1990s was the British Library at St Pancras, designed by Colin St John Wilson, a pupil and associate of Sir Leslie Martin (with whom he won the original commission – in 1962 – to rehouse the library on a site south of the British Museum). The site at St Pancras, in a drab and crime-ridden quarter close to two rail terminals, was acquired in the 1970s, but Wilson's building was completed and occupied only in 1997. For the Prince of Wales, it resembled "an academy for secret policemen". For most architects and critics, the building was simply an irrelevance, for all the admirable heroism of its architect's struggle to see it built – its rehash of Aalto-esque and Wrightian themes and desperate urge to relate to the context of Gilbert Scott's Gothic Revival St Pancras Hotel found few echoes on the contemporary scene. It did not help that during the 1980s red brick and pitched roofs had become the staple vocabulary of suburban superstore design. Set back from the busy Euston Road behind a bleak paved square and externally inscrutable, the library does not look inviting. The interior is, however, admirable for the generosity of its public spaces and the high quality of its detailing – it would be hard to argue that Wilson's long struggle was in vain. In the age of the private finance initiative schemes promoted equally by the Tories and New Labour, it seemed unlikely that a public building of such obsessive quality would be commissioned for London again.

Rogers and Foster had famously prospered on overseas jobs during the 1970s and 1980s, with relatively little work in Britain. Foster had suffered the cancellation of two exceptional projects: the Hammersmith transport interchange of 1978, which would have turned a polluted backwater into a hub for the capital (the scheme was cancelled and Hammersmith sank further into the mire) and the BBC headquarters scheme of 1982, abandoned by an organization with grand ambitions but no real vision or sense of purpose. The Channel 4 building, completed in 1994, could be seen as a typical Rogers commission, tuned to the specific needs of an end-user with more drive than the hapless BBC, and drawing on the vocabulary of Lloyd's. The redesigned project for the Daiwa site (pp. 240–41) saw Rogers working with a design-and-build contract and a brief for speculative office space – to produce, against all the odds, one of the most distinctive of new City buildings. For Lloyd's Register of Shipping, Rogers slotted a new, low-energy building into

a constrained historic site at Fenchurch Street – only the City's crass insistence that an unlisted building be retained, and the new development thus be denied any street presence, marred this subtle exercise in balancing conservation and radical new design. The radical and exploratory instincts that have permeated Rogers's work over the last forty years emerged strongly at the Millennium Dome, a highly appropriate and economical – as well as spectacular – container for the Millennium Experience at the Greenwich Peninsula on which Rogers's partner Mike Davies worked with Buro Happold engineers. Other big names were involved in the design of the Dome's zones – Zaha Hadid, Branson Coates and Eva Jiricna included – but the demolition of the interior, months after the closure of the Experience, provided a strange echo of the events of 1951. Despite an attendance of twelve million, the project had been deemed a failure, and the government was anxious to erase its memory and dispose of the Dome. (At the time of writing, its fate remains uncertain.) Foster and Partners' emergence as a mainstream commercial architectural practice was all the more striking, with half a dozen City projects in hand by 2001. Foster's willingness to embrace quantity alongside quality was seen by some as a worrying trend – yet Foster trounced his critics with the exceptionally innovative designs for the Swiss Re Tower (see pp. 232–33), designed to replace the ruins of the Baltic Exchange, wrecked by an IRA bomb, and given planning consent amid bitter controversy. More than Seifert in the 1960s or Farrell in the 1980s, Foster was omnipresent in the London of the millennium, dominating the world of civic and cultural, as well as commercial, design. Swiss Re, incorporating radical new ideas on servicing and the environment, has its roots in innovative projects such as Willis Faber and even the very early schemes done for Fred Olsen. In contrast, Foster's British Museum Great Court (see pp. 68–69) is both modern and monumental, taking its cue, perhaps, from I.M. Pei's work at the National Gallery in Washington, DC, and the Louvre. Swiss Re is significant not just for its memorable form, but also for its progressive environmental agenda. The recession of the 1990s had done little, in the absence of legislation, to persuade British developers and architects of the necessity of a move towards 'green' buildings – a well-researched and entirely practical project such as Future Systems' Green Office was dismissed as an idealistic gesture. In this area of design, as in many others, London's outlook was closer to that of New York than Frankfurt. Only slowly did British attitudes to environmental design change.

The Mound Stand at Lord's cricket ground, designed by Foster's former partner Michael Hopkins, was a popular success in the 1980s, combining traditional and modern materials – brick, steel and PVC-coated fabric – to produce a building with a strong identity and sense of place. Here, as at Glyndebourne, Hopkins transformed the image of an old-established institution. (At Lord's, he was followed by Nicholas Grimshaw and Future Systems, which designed the Media Centre, one of the most potent images of modern London – see pp. 96–97.) But Hopkins's greatest challenge came with the 1992 commission for an extension to the Palace of Westminster to house MPs' offices, committee rooms and other facilities for the House of Commons. The new building, subsequently named Portcullis House (see pp. 230–31), forms a structurally integrated whole with the new Westminster Underground station that lies below it (see pp. 50–51), but while the station is an awesome work of engineering, Portcullis House is a carefully considered exercise in contextual Modernism. Creating a building with a strong identity of its own that neither defers to nor contends with Barry's magnificent Gothic complex was a huge challenge. Seen from the South Bank, or glimpsed from Marks Barfield's London Eye (see pp.82–83), the success of the scheme is clear, and, though the façades are perhaps over-detailed, the sheer bravado of the skyline, with its boldly industrial chimneys, commands respect; only Hopkins, perhaps, could have produced this confident dialogue with history. But it is the glazed central court, with its finely crafted roof structure of concrete, steel and laminated timber, that is the spectacular heart of the building – sadly one that is largely inaccessible to the electorate. Hopkins's recasting of the face of modern architecture was based on a real dialogue with tradition, not in terms of style but of materials and technologies. His quest for a new way is widely misunderstood, most often as a compromise with historicism, whereas Hopkins's radicalism lies in his ability to get to the roots of tradition, which, as T.S. Eliot insisted, "cannot be inherited ... if you want it you must obtain it by great labour". Hopkins's labour continues.

Nicholas Grimshaw's stand at Lord's was one of a

Opposite
Michael Hopkins's station at Westminster is one of the major sights of the Jubilee line extension, which became a showcase for new British architecture.

Left
The Queen Elizabeth II Great Court at the British Museum symbolizes Norman Foster's dominant position on the British architectural scene at the beginning of the twenty-first century.

number of London buildings of the 1980s and 1990s by his practice, of which the most widely acclaimed was the Waterloo Terminal. Grimshaw's continued attachment to the machine aesthetic and his fascination with metallic construction (and reluctance to embrace a wider palette of materials) may have limited his appeal to commercial and public clients. His supermarket in Camden Town was a trailblazer for better retail architecture, though some considered its austere vocabulary inappropriate for the function of the building.

As Foster, Rogers, Hopkins and Grimshaw, all well into their sixties by the year 2000, reinforced their grip on the London scene, younger practices moved into the front rank. Among them were Wilkinson Eyre, largely on the basis of its work for the Jubilee line extension; Lifschutz Davidson and John McAslan, the most successful of the 1980s practices with roots in the Foster–Rogers circle; and Allies & Morrison, a practice with a feeling for history and a fastidious and refined approach, forged in the Cambridge tradition of Leslie Martin, which has won it work in a remarkable range of contexts. Rick Mather is an architect of an older generation whose London work up to the 1990s consisted largely of restaurants, shops and domestic interiors, plus a solitary office scheme in Docklands. In addition to his work as masterplanner for the South Bank, Mather has recently become identified with major refurbishments to leading museums, which include the National Maritime (see pp.64–65), Wallace Collection (see pp.74–75) and – the most accomplished of this series of projects – Soane's much-imitated Dulwich Picture Gallery (see pp. 58–59). Even more striking was the advance of Will Alsop into the inner circle at the turn of the millennium. Alsop's early projects, carried out in partnership with John Lyall, were modest but highly original – the low-cost reworking of Tottenham Hale station is a good example. North Greenwich station (see pp. 40–41) demonstrated his skill at creating memorable form and using colour to dramatize it. Peckham Library (see pp. 98–99) applied this skill to civic ends – the library was one element in a new public space at the heart of the district. Its impact on Peckham was comparable to that of Owen Williams's Pioneer Health Centre seventy years earlier – Alsop caught the mood of the local community, with its longing for change and improvement. Peckham Library was an appropriate choice for the RIBA's Stirling Prize at the end of 2000, since it symbolized the mood of renewal and regeneration in areas that had missed out on the commercial bonanza of the 1980s and reflected, in particular, the remarkable transformation of

Southwark. Having seen major transport projects, including stations for Thameslink and Crossrail, slip from his grasp, Alsop has moved since 2000 into the commercial field with office projects in Southwark and the City, the latter involving an operation of urban repair for a quarter devastated by insensate 1960s planning, though his inspirational proposals for the reconstruction of the BBC's landmark site at Portland Place proved too radical for the corporation, which has since appointed MacCormac Jamieson Prichard.

Alsop's new prominence on the London scene contrasted with the marked absence of projects by other innovative figures of his generation such as David Chipperfield, Zaha Hadid and Nigel Coates, all of whom have made London their base for international careers. Though Branson Coates completed an extension to the Geffrye Museum in 1998, most of its work in London has taken the form of interiors, including important retail commissions. Chipperfield's most significant London commission to date is a fit-out at the Natural History Museum, though, like Hadid, he is involved in major foreign projects. The architectural culture of London is strong, rooted in a lively critical discourse and in architectural schools of global reputation. Hadid's career was one of many launched at the Architectural Association under the leadership of Alvin Boyarsky; winner of the Pritzker Prize for Architecture in the United States in 2004, Hadid won the competition in 2005 to design the new headquarters in London of the Architecture Foundation. Tony Fretton, another Architectural Association-bred talent, was another whose projects were lamentably under-built, though his Lisson Gallery is a miniature gem and his 2001 town house in Chelsea (see pp. 168–69) a remarkable and uncommon instance of a modern house located not in a suburban grove but on a historic central London street.

The neglect of talents of this magnitude does not reflect well on London, yet a score or more of outstanding young practices moved on during the 1990s from the shop fit-outs, bars, restaurants and small domestic commissions that are the mainstay of a rising generation to much more substantial jobs. They included Allford Hall Monaghan Morris, Buschow Henley, Cartwright Pickard, Harper Mackay, Haworth Tompkins, Proctor Matthews, Rivington Street Studio, Tim Ronalds, and Walters & Cohen, with the names of David Adjaye, Jo Hagan, Softroom, Shed 54, Wells Mackereth and Foreign Office Architects all well tipped for solid success in the coming decade.

London's architects thrived in the context of renewed economic growth from the mid-1990s onwards. The new

Victoria Miro Gallery is one of several commercial art galleries to have moved around the turn of the millennium from relatively cramped premises in London's traditional art quarter around Bond Street to far loftier spaces in the East End, where former warehouses are regularly being converted for new uses.

century was heralded by a move to build high. Apart from Foster's Swiss Re, plans for new office towers at Bishopsgate (Kohn Pedersen Fox; see pp. 200–01), Fenchurch Street (Wilkinson Eyre) and London Bridge (Renzo Piano Building Workshop/Broadway Malyan; pp 218–19) were announced, with Marks Barfield, buoyed by the triumphant success of the London Eye, floating the idea of a mixed-use high-rise, with a strong element of rented housing, for a site as yet unspecified. Arup Associates designed a high-rise replacement for Plantation House in Fenchurch Street, a huge 1930s classical office scheme that was the subject of a £20,000,000 rehab completed in 1992 – seven years later, the whole building was flattened. By early 2001 the issue of high buildings had polarized opinion to a degree reminiscent of the 1980s – the tragic events of 9/11 seemed briefly to cast doubt on the future of the tall building. English Heritage, backed by a coalition of amenity groups, led the anti-tower lobby, arguing, against the evidence of recent history, that London should remain a low/medium rise conurbation. For Mayor Ken Livingstone, well-sited, high-quality towers were a symbol of the dynamic social and economic life of London. Livingstone's support provoked the government to adopt a generally negative line, despite the supportive stance of the Commission for Architecture and the Built Environment, CABE – the Blair government's replacement for the abolished Royal Fine Art Commission. Local authorities were divided: Westminster, Tory-controlled and supposedly pro-enterprise, dithered and sought to limit new buildings to a height of no more than 100 metres. The City, ever aware of the threat of Docklands and Europe, was more receptive, as were the inner-London boroughs, such as Southwark, for which regeneration and job creation were priorities.

London in the early twenty-first century is a city of *grands projets*, both completed (Tate Modern, the Great Court, the Royal Opera House, Somerset House and the pedestrianization of the north side of Trafalgar Square) and forthcoming (Wembley Stadium and the National Athletics Stadium among them). The oft-quoted contrast between "private affluence and public squalor" is less apparent than it was two decades back and public (albeit Lottery) money has renewed much of the capital's cultural infrastructure. Yet London's *petits projets* are equally significant in the continuing restructuring of the metropolis. The art world, for example, moved eastwards and southwards. Paxton Locher's Jerwood Space inhabits a radical reworking of a Victorian school in Southwark. Other galleries moved to Hoxton and Shoreditch. The former hydraulic power station

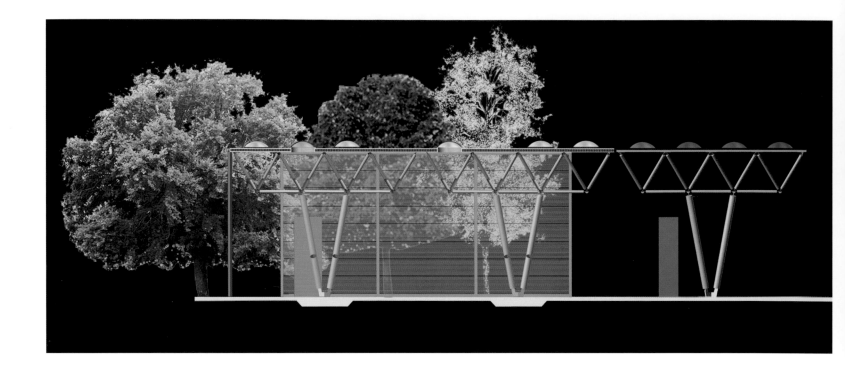

close to the Thames at Wapping opened in autumn 2000 as a new visual and performing-arts centre with fit-out by Joshua Wright of Shed 54. Artists and craftspeople colonized the great undercroft of the former Bishopsgate goods station in Shoreditch, site for an abortive tower project of the 1980s. The Victoria Miro Gallery moved from Cork Street to Wharf Road, N1. The idea of reinhabiting and redefining areas of the city was hardly a novelty – in the 1950s Notting Hill was a near-slum, Clerkenwell and Bankside were industrial quarters – but the push into the former industrial fringes produced a real architectural challenge. Buschow Henley addressed the issue of reuse in their mixed-use development at Shepherdess Walk, Hackney (see pp. 184–85), while Cartwright Pickard's housing at nearby Murray Grove (see pp. 180–81) sought a new contextual modern vocabulary while utilizing prefabricated components for speed and economy of construction. At the Greenwich Peninsula, within sight of the Dome, Proctor Matthews's housing for the Millennium Village (see pp. 178–79) , colourful and strongly articulated, blazed the regeneration trail amidst a sea of mud and dereliction – the project was an act of faith in what could one day be a vibrant new district. After twenty or more years, during which the social housing stock diminished by nearly a quarter, the rented sector is back, with new agencies (such as the Poplar

Housing and Regeneration Community Association, responsible for 4000 dwellings in the East End, or the Stonebridge Housing Action Trust) replacing local authorities as landlords and voluntary associations and trusts (such as Peabody) playing a revitalized role and addressing the needs of a varied clientele badly served by traditional council housing. For the first time in decades, new schools and medical centres command attention as architecture; practices such as Penoyre & Prasad and Avanti Architects have a notable record in this area, while Guy Greenfield's medical centre at Hammersmith (see pp. 128–29) is a striking landmark as well as an outstanding community amenity. New public open spaces, such as the extended and transformed Mile End Park (see pp. 32–33), with its Green Bridge by Piers Gough, and Patel Taylor's Thames Barrier Park (see pp. 48–49), the first entirely new park established in London since the Second World War, have provided a latter-day interpretation of the public park of the nineteenth century. Culture projects downsized after the spending splurge that followed the launch of the Lottery. English National Opera has completed a sensible and respectful refurbishment scheme at the London Coliseum, having earlier abandoned ideas of a new opera house on another site. Tim Ronalds's reconstruction of the Hackney Empire has the attraction of catering for a far from élitist East End

The cardboard pavilion by Shigeru Ban Architects and Gumuchdjian Associates, planned for Kew Gardens, reflects new approaches to building technology and the environment.

audience. As the rather mixed record of the Royal Opera House since its £200,000,000 makeover suggests, costly buildings do not necessarily produce great performances.

London architecture today is, on the one hand, a reassertion of the continuity of the city, on the other, a manifesto for radical change. Some were critical of the preponderance of conversion and reuse schemes among London's millennium projects, yet the background was a long period in which historic buildings and areas were wantonly destroyed – the whole of the London Docks, for example, vanished in the 1970s. It was against this background that the journalist Marcus Binney and a group of friends formed SAVE Britain's Heritage in 1975 – European Architectural Heritage Year. SAVE had its roots in the movement to rescue threatened country houses, but soon became embroiled in London issues. Its influence was critical in the reprieves granted to Battersea Power Station and the old Billingsgate Market (subsequently converted to a dealing floor by Richard Rogers) and in the defeat of Peter Palumbo's Mansion House Square. SAVE worked with Terry Farrell, an architect with a sure feel for combining old and new, on an alternative scheme for Palumbo's site on Poultry, only to see it eventually razed for James Stirling's Number 1 Poultry.

SAVE and the other amenity bodies, including the fledgling Twentieth Century Society, informed a steady move towards the recognition of old buildings of quality as a resource. By 2000, applications to totally demolish listed buildings in London were rare. Increasingly architects have the task of adapting not just Georgian and Victorian buildings, but also those of twentieth-century heritage, to twenty-first-century needs. Denys Lasdun's Keeling House, designed with a working-class community of the 1950s in mind, has been reborn, after years of dereliction, as an oasis of chic living (see pp. 172–73). Erno Goldfinger's iconic Trellick Tower in north Kensington became a fashionable address, and Alexander Fleming House, the Perret inspired office scheme he designed at the Elephant & Castle, was reprieved from demolition and converted into apartments for affluent young City professionals. Paul Hamilton's Paddington maintenance depot is now the headquarters of a retail group. Even Highbury Stadium, if and when Arsenal Football Club moves to a new site, could be converted to housing (see pp. 152–53). And Battersea Power Station, left beached and apparently doomed by the failure of a 1980s leisure project, may soon be brought to life as a spectacular auditorium (see pp. 80–81).

At the same time, London architecture pushes constantly forward, generating not only new talents but also new ideas on a scale that neither contemporary New York nor Tokyo can match. Wigglesworth & Till's Straw House and Quilted Office (see pp. 186–87), 'green' but immensely stylish, Shigeru Ban Architects and Gumuchdjian Associates' pavilion of cardboard, planned for Kew Gardens, and David Adjaye's Elektra House (see p. 162) represent new London architecture at the cutting edge. The talents of the future are making their mark, as ever, in bar fit-outs, flat conversions and house extensions – the kind of job that Rogers and Foster's Team 4 was agonizing over forty years ago. Mass-housing developers now routinely commission schemes that, a decade ago, would have seemed impossibly leading edge and unsaleable (even if they were to gain planning consent). Perhaps it is the shift towards the public domain and towards a balance between social and commercial gain that has made Londoners look at architecture and architects – and even developers – in a less cynical light. London is even now not the grandest of the world's capitals. As Ian Nairn wrote in 1964, "it does not make a display of its best things".[7] Ordinariness is steadily becoming a rare quality as the tide of growth and investment, and the fame conferred by literature and films, permeates even the more obscure parts of the capital – how long before Hugh Grant stars in a romantic drama set in Neasden or Catford? Yet London is increasingly a place where old and new architecture are welded into livable spaces, where history and modernity coexist and feed on each other. As such it has lessons to teach the world.

1   Richard Rogers (with Mark Fisher), *A New London,* London 1992, p. xliv.

2   See R. Burdett (ed.), *City Changes: Architecture in the City of London, 1985–95,* London 1992.

3   S. Hardingham, *London: A Guide to Recent Architecture,* 4th edn, London 1999, p. 310.

4   I. Nairn, *Modern Buildings in London,* London 1964, foreword.

5   C. Jencks (ed.), *Post Modern Triumphs in London,* Architectural Design Profile 91, London 1991, pp. 12–13: a remarkably well documented account of Postmodernism in London, with all the major projects illustrated.

6   Rogers (with Fisher), *op. cit.,* p. 51, note 1.

7   Nairn, *op. cit.,* foreword, note 4.

BERMONDSEY UNDERGROUND STATION
IAN RITCHIE ARCHITECTS

CANARY WHARF UNDERGROUND STATION
FOSTER AND PARTNERS

GREEN BRIDGE/MILE END PARK
CZWG ARCHITECTS/TIBBALDS TM2/COMMUNITY LAND USE

HUNGERFORD BRIDGE
LIFSCHUTZ DAVIDSON

MILLENNIUM BRIDGE
FOSTER AND PARTNERS

MILLENNIUM DOME
RICHARD ROGERS PARTNERSHIP/BURO HAPPOLD/IMAGINATION

NORTH GREENWICH STATION
ALSOP, LYALL & STORMER;
WITH TRANSPORT INTERCHANGE: FOSTER AND PARTNERS

SOMERSET HOUSE
PETER INSKIP & PETER JENKINS; DONALD INSALL ASSOCIATES;
JEREMY DIXON.EDWARD JONES

SOUTHWARK UNDERGROUND STATION
MacCORMAC JAMIESON PRICHARD

STRATFORD REGIONAL STATION
WILKINSON EYRE/TROUGHTON McASLAN

THAMES BARRIER PARK
PATEL TAYLOR ARCHITECTS/GROUP SIGNES/OVE ARUP & PARTNERS

WESTMINSTER UNDERGROUND STATION
MICHAEL HOPKINS & PARTNERS

WORLD SQUARES FOR ALL
FOSTER AND PARTNERS

BERMONDSEY UNDERGROUND STATION
JAMAICA ROAD, SE1

IAN RITCHIE ARCHITECTS, 1990–2000

The Jubilee line extension project produced a number of stations – Canary Wharf, North Greenwich and Westminster included – that are major architectural landmarks set at key points on the route. Ian Ritchie's Bermondsey is rather different. It sits alongside the bleak, heavily trafficked Jamaica Road, serving an area of south-east London that is far from gentrified. Indeed, there were doubts as to the need for a station at this point – intensive political lobbying was necessary to quash the threat of cancellation.

The route of the Jubilee line extension from London Bridge to Bermondsey follows the line of the 878-arch viaduct that carried the 1836 London & Greenwich Railway, arguably the world's first rapid-transit system, into London Bridge.

Ian Ritchie, one of the first architects to be considered for a commission for the Jubilee line extension, took on the Bermondsey job in 1990. The brief was to provide a local station, the equivalent of Charles Holden's street-corner stations on the Northern line, with few frills. It was assumed that offices or a residential development might eventually be built over the station, but the demand for either would follow on from the opening of the extension. The site was complicated by its proximity to

a major road and by waterlogged soil conditions (in the eighteenth century Bermondsey had been a spa).

The completed station is distinguished by its directness and calm logic. The sunlit booking hall is entered directly from the street. The escalators extend downwards at right angles to the platforms, with natural light flooding into the great concrete box sunk into the wet clay. (In a Holden station, the escalators would be contained within tubes and there would be no natural light.) The aesthetic of the station is formed by the contrast between rough and finely finished concrete – seen in the 'blades' that provide structural support for the box – and by the "jewellery", as Ritchie describes the fit-out, which includes blue-glass benches on the platforms.

Bermondsey builds on the Hong Kong model brought to London by Roland Paoletti and transforms it into a lightweight but robust balance of engineering and architecture. At Bermondsey, the promise of the Jubilee line extension as a force for regeneration is fully realized. Like the slum churches of the nineteenth century, this is a work of art done for a poor neighbourhood – one that is already benefiting from the dynamic impact of the Underground.

Above
Platform level, with the concrete structure powerfully expressed.

Opposite
Ticket hall, brilliantly daylit with a clear route from the street.

Platform, with blue-glass benches designed by the architects.

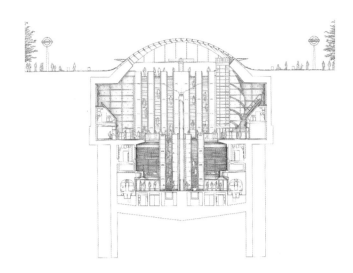

CANARY WHARF UNDERGROUND STATION, E14

FOSTER AND PARTNERS, 1990–2000

Canary Wharf station has the grandeur of a mainline rail terminal and the sleekness of an international airport, embodying all the expertise that Foster and Partners have developed in the design of public buildings and infrastructure over the last thirty years. Yet, for all its monumental grandeur, Canary Wharf is a link in the chain of the Jubilee line extension (Green Park to Stratford), one of a series of eleven new (or largely rebuilt) stations commissioned by the extension's architect-in-chief, Roland Paoletti.

Work on developing the Canary Wharf 'office city' began in 1987, and the buildings began to come on stream on the eve of the 1990s recession. By 1999, however, the project housed 25,000 workers – within a few years, this figure was to more than double. As existing transport connections, notably the Docklands Light Railway, were stretched to breaking point, the Jubilee line extension link arrived in the nick of time. The new station was designed to cope with future growth (40,000 passengers hourly) but could soon be working at capacity.

The site for the station was a former dock basin just south of Canada Square, the heart of Canary Wharf. A huge concrete box, 300 metres long, contained within diaphragm walls, was sunk into the drained dock and rooted into the waterlogged ground with deep piles. On top of the station box, a new park was created – a valuable amenity but also a vital practical device to prevent the station floating

upwards. If the engineering achievement involved in the project was heroic, it is the potency of the architectural expression, however, that places Canary Wharf firmly among Foster's major works (where his other recent works at Canary Wharf regrettably do not belong).

Externally the station has a discreet presence – the glazed entrance canopies are a development of those Foster designed for the Bilbao metro system. The experience of descending the banks of escalators into the 265-metre-long concourse is as memorable as any found in contemporary London architecture. Natural light floods into the space and there is a clear and direct route down to the platform level. Ticket offices and other service spaces are rigorously marshalled along the sides of the concourse and lighting and other services effortlessly integrated. The lightness of the architecture is astounding, considering the demands on the structure. Slim, elliptical columns support the roof, from which a mezzanine level is suspended. Architecture and engineering are, in the great Foster tradition, in complete harmony. One of the remarkable features of the Jubilee line extension is the variety of its stations – Southwark is complex and reflective, North Greenwich expansive and populist. Canary Wharf triumphs through sheer rationality – the inevitability of function expressed in noble form. The miseries of Camden Town or Tottenham Court Road seem part of another world.

Above
Cross section, showing structure sunk into former dock.

Station entrance, with glazed canopy illuminating the escalators.

The station's majestic concourse level.

Opposite
From the platform level there is a clear and daylit route towards the exit.

West Plaza
Canary Wharf **DOCKLANDS** LIGHT RAIL

GREEN BRIDGE/MILE END PARK
MILE END ROAD, E3

CZWG ARCHITECTS/TIBBALDS TM2/COMMUNITY LAND USE
1995–2001

In comparison with other leading European cities, London has been slow to create new urban parks – in spite of the fact that the public park was pioneered in Britain. The Mile End Park is not entirely new. An open space was created here by the GLC in the aftermath of the wartime bombing that wrecked much of the surrounding area, leaving swathes of devastation. The 364,221-square-metre park extended south of Victoria Park towards the Thames, along the Grand Union Canal. It was an heroic effort, though the open space was seriously compromised and compartmented by roads and railways and by a local authority decision not to proceed with the demolition of an area of housing close to its heart. The

initial enthusiasm with which the scheme was implemented seems to have subsequently evaporated: in recent years, the landscape has been under-maintained, threadbare and, in places, unsavoury. A masterplan for, in effect, re-creating the park as a variegated landscape catering for the community and providing sports and play areas, quiet planted zones, an ecology park and areas for public art was published in 1995 after extensive public consultation. Supported by the local authority, business and community interests, it was implemented over the next six years with funding from various sources, including the Millennium Commission. There are now seven distinct areas reflecting themes of

play, art, ecology, sport and fun, the whole being managed by an independent trust.

Mile End Road is virtually the midway point in the park's north–south run, a very busy traffic artery that needed to be bridged if the coherence of the landscape was to be maintained. A simple pedestrian bridge would hardly have addressed this issue. Instead, Piers Gough of CZWG had the idea of "mending" the hole in the park by building a planted link across the road. Gough was in some ways an obvious choice for this commission: his architecture is famed for its qualities of wit and accessibility, though, sadly, he has not won the major public jobs that he deserves. (Perhaps his most famous work is the

public lavatory/flower shop in Westbourne Grove, completed in 1993.) Constructed in 1998–2000, the 25-metre-wide Green Bridge reads as a natural continuation of the landscape – "you don't need to show people how it stands up", says Gough. "The point is the grass and trees, not the engineering." The bridge, carrying pedestrian and cycle routes, manages to be substantial and shapely, a piece of living urban sculpture. One drawback of wide bridges across roads – think of the typical Victorian railway bridge – is that they create dank and gloomy areas at street level. Gough addressed this issue by locating shops under the span, also providing valuable income for the new trust.

Opposite and below
The bridge is a vital link across the traffic-choked
Mile End Road, connecting two sections of a
linear urban park.

HUNGERFORD BRIDGE, WC2/SE1

LIFSCHUTZ DAVIDSON, 1996–2002

Hungerford Railway Bridge is widely regarded as one of the worst eyesores in London – yet it seems destined to survive for many years to come. In 1986 Richard Rogers's visionary 'London as it could be' project proposed to remove the heavy and utilitarian Victorian railway bridge (which replaced an elegant suspension bridge by Brunel) and to replace it with a lightweight structure carrying a footbridge and monorail link, with the existing Charing Cross station closed. Terry Farrell's Embankment Place scheme subsequently cemented the station in place by covering the tracks with profitable office space, though the opening of the Jubilee line link to London Bridge and Waterloo makes Charing Cross an even more superfluous terminal.

Lifschutz Davidson's scheme, designed with structural engineers WSP, seeks to make the best use of the elephantine nineteenth-century structure, which carried a narrow pedestrian walkway on its eastern edge. Two new bridges (officially called the Golden Jubilee Bridges) are attached to the existing bridge on its eastern and western flanks, so that, for the first time, pedestrians are able to enjoy a view of Westminster from the Hungerford Bridge. The structural approach is as economical as that of the Victorians was cumbrous, and it evokes the spirit of Brunel and the 1951 Festival of Britain. (The project was generated by the ongoing campaign to revitalize the South Bank arts centre site and to improve its connections to central London.) The *in situ* concrete bridge decks are suspended on supporting steel rods from inclined 26.5-metre steel pylons sunk into the river bed. On the south side of the river, the bridge decks link directly to the terraces of the Royal Festival Hall.

Pragmatic rather than visionary, this project addresses a practical issue – that of encouraging people to cross to the South Bank – in a straightforward, but incisive fashion. But the issue of Charing Cross remains: one day it should be closed and the tracks across the Thames torn up.

MILLENNIUM BRIDGE, EC4/SE1

FOSTER AND PARTNERS, 1996–2001

Norman Foster's victory in the competition for this new bridge, connecting St Paul's and the City with the new Tate Modern, seemed effortless, part of his sure hold on key London millennium projects. The Millennium Bridge project was developed in collaboration with Ove Arup & Partners and the eminent sculptor Sir Anthony Caro. The bridge was scheduled to open early in 2000, to service the new Tate. It did open – for a weekend – but was then closed for more than a year to enable significant technical adjustments to be carried out to counter a pronounced wobble that occurred when large numbers of people crossed it on its inaugural weekend. Foster's detractors crowed and there was an element of *Schadenfreude* in some of the other criticisms made of the scheme.

Yet the problems of the bridge flowed from the high technical and aesthetic ambitions that underlay the project. This was to be the first new Thames crossing since the completion of Tower Bridge over a century ago and the first Thames bridge ever set aside purely for the use of pedestrians. The Thames is a big river, far

wider as it runs through the City towards the sea than Dublin's Liffey or Paris's Seine. Foster's design capitalized on the thrill of being suspended high above the water, in the midst of a 320-metre span. The basic form is that of a suspension bridge, with two Y-shaped armatures supporting cables that run alongside the 4-metre wide aluminium deck, which is engaged by means of steel transverse arms. The cables rise no more than 2.3 metres above the deck, so that the effect is very different from that of the typical suspension bridge – Foster aimed at a thin ribbon of metal, a direct statement of the act of bridging the water. By night, the goal was to make the bridge a blade of light. By these means, those using the bridge were guaranteed uninterrupted views along the river, while the slenderness of the structure addressed the criticisms of those who feared that it would intrude into those precious views. In the quest of maximum structural economy, the design was finely tuned, perhaps too much so. Foster's daring has, however, been vindicated, now that the bridge has successfuly been brought into use.

Above
The bridge links the City and St Paul's Cathedral with the regenerated Bankside area around Tate Modern.

Structural detail, with view up river towards Blackfriars.

Opposite
The spare structure of the bridge has a sculptural elegance that contrasts with the solidity of Tate Modern.

MILLENNIUM DOME
GREENWICH PENINSULA, SE10
RICHARD ROGERS PARTNERSHIP/BURO
HAPPOLD/IMAGINATION, 1996–2000

The Dome achieved more media coverage and generated more political and public debate than any British building of the last one hundred years. One needs to look back to the 1851 Crystal Palace to find a parallel. The Crystal Palace was widely derided and the 1951 Festival of Britain was disowned, and then demolished, by an incoming Tory government, yet both have gone down in history as successful ventures. In contrast, the Dome has been seen as something of a failure. At the time of writing its future remains uncertain; the zones and other internal elements that accounted for most of the total project cost of around £760,000,000 have been destroyed.

In itself, however, the Dome is a straightforward, low-cost (£40,000,000 for 80,000 square metres of space) structure ideally suited to the brief of accommodating large numbers of visitors (up to 35,000 a day were expected) and housing static exhibits and live events and with potential for continued use – the would-be users exist, if the political will exists to keep the Dome standing.

The origins of the Dome extend back into the early 1990s when the John Major government decided to set up the Millennium Commission as a recipient of

funds from the new National Lottery. In 1996 the former gasworks site at Greenwich was chosen as the site for the Millennium Festival, with Imagination given the task of developing plans for the project. Richard Rogers, then working on a masterplan for the whole peninsula, was brought in to design the architectural setting. The idea of a masted, cable-stayed, fabric-covered structure was developed by Richard Rogers Partnership director Mike Davies, building on previous schemes by the practice, and engineers Buro Happold were enlisted to provide a structural agenda. Work began on site in summer 1997, and the Dome was ready for an official opening on New Year's Eve 1999.

With the zones (including structures by Branson Coates, Zaha Hadid and Eva Jiricna) stripped out, the Dome has once again become a grand empty space, served by a fine, and currently underused, transport interchange and a fast Underground link to central London. The structure is good for half a century and the fabric cladding should last twenty-five years: dismantling the Dome would represent a sad and wasteful end to the saga of the Millennium Experience.

Right
Interior view, showing the Talk Zone, now dismantled.

The structure, seen here at night, has become a prominent East End landmark.

Opposite
Detail, showing the masted, cable-stayed, fabric-covered structure and one of the brightly coloured service drums.

Opposite
The industrial aesthetic of the service staircase contrasts with the backlit cobalt-blue glass wall behind.

Below
The blue motif is continued in the mosaic applied to the wall surfaces and V-shaped columns.

At platform level the underbelly of the passenger concourse is clearly visible.

The integrated transport facility at North Greenwich was planned and commenced long before the emergence of plans for the Millennium Festival and Dome in 1996. Initially, the new station was intended to serve Port Greenwich, a huge residential and commercial development by British Gas of the former gasworks site on the Greenwich Peninsula, but the project fell victim to the 1990s recession and was never resurrected. The decision to proceed with the Jubilee line extension connection was fortuitous – it made the Dome possible and will serve as the hub for the future regeneration of the peninsula (which is already under way) and for public transport links to a wide swathe of south-east London and north Kent.

Will Alsop, then working with his former partner John Lyall, was approached in 1990 to develop proposals for one of the largest stations on the extension: the completed station is 358 metres long with three platforms. The practice developed the project with engineers Robert Benaim & Associates, with detailed design development and construction overseen by Roland Paoletti's in-house team. However, the station bears all the marks of Alsop's approach: colourful, strongly modelled, flamboyant and with a potent popular appeal – it is probably the Jubilee line extension station that has won the most plaudits from the travelling public.

The first idea was to build a station in an open cutting, surrounded by a green square and with the concourse suspended in the void. It would have been stunning, but the decision was made to give the station a lid. Construction began in 1995. The original concept was developed in the revised scheme, with the ticket hall becoming a great steel-clad 'boat' hanging in space, with views down to the platforms, which are accommodated within a spectacular train hall. The roof is supported on 21 pairs of 13-metre high *in situ* concrete columns in V formations, clad in blue mosaic. A huge wall of backlit cobalt blue glass provides intriguing reflections of escalators, people and trains.

The station has no expression at ground level. The logical course might have been to commission the surface-level bus station from the same architects, but it went to Norman Foster as late as 1996 and was built in little more than a year. Tony Hunt's structure cantilevers off column supports on the edge of the station, with the 6500-square-metre roof supported on steel 'trees'. The image is that of a great bird. Though Foster and Alsop have a very different approach, their respective contributions at North Greenwich work well together and the bus station, along with that at Canada Water designed by Eva Jiricna, represents a move towards civilizing travel conditions for London's long-suffering bus users.

SOMERSET HOUSE, STRAND, WC2

PETER INSKIP & PETER JENKINS; DONALD INSALL
ASSOCIATES; JEREMY DIXON.EDWARD JONES, 1996–2001

Like the British Museum's Great Court (see pp. 68–69), the Somerset House project is about turning underused, private spaces into a major extension of the public domain. London is a city where, beyond the green expanses of the Royal Parks, there are few oases of quiet away from the noise of the streets; the squares of the West End, for example, were traditionally private places. The project has also created impressive new spaces for the display of works of art, making Somerset House the nucleus of a new cultural and educational campus.

Somerset House was never strictly a public building. Sir William Chambers's monumental complex looks like a royal palace but was intended as offices for civil servants, with the fine rooms along the Strand frontage as accommodation for the newly constituted Royal Academy and Society of Antiquaries (which subsequently moved to Burlington House). There were no other grand interiors and the impressive central court and riverside terrace were used only by those who worked or (in the case of the Navy commissioners) lived in Somerset House. Chambers's grand plan was completed long after his death with the construction of new wings to the east (for King's College, which opened in 1829) and to the west (designed by Sir James Pennethorne in 1856 for the Inland Revenue).

London University's Courtauld Institute and Galleries moved to Somerset House in 1990, occupying the fine rooms and other spaces along the Strand frontage. The

Somerset House Trust was established in 1997 with the aim of gradually bringing the remainder of the site into public use as, potentially, London's Louvre. By the end of 2000, a series of major elements within the overall masterplan had been achieved. Inskip & Jenkins's galleries for the Gilbert Collection occupy the monumental spaces below the riverside terrace and part of the basement of the South Building and can be accessed via Chambers's Great Arch – once a water gate, but now beached on the Embankment – as well as from the Great Court. Inskip & Jenkins's design strategy combines careful restoration of the original structure with unequivocally contemporary interventions in a broadly high-tech manner. The economy of this approach provides an appropriate showcase for an extraordinary range of objects, ranging from the exquisite to the kitsch.

Donald Insall Associates' reworking of the Great Court included major below-ground works – lavatories are provided, for example, for large audiences attending open-air concerts – as well as the resurfacing of the court with setts, replacing institutional asphalt on what was a civil service car park. In the South Building, a restaurant, bar and shops have been provided as well as galleries displaying a rotating selection of works from St Petersburg's Hermitage Museum. Dixon.Jones's fountain, which forms the magical centrepiece of the Great Court, was commissioned in 1998, and its

choreographed battery of fifty-five water jets is a stunning invention, enjoyable and elegant. Less successful is the same firm's terrace café: its mannered woven acrylic canopies are flimsy on a windy spring day, and the bridge link between the riverside terrace and Waterloo Bridge shows little regard for the geometries of Giles Scott's bridge abutments.

The Inland Revenue continues to occupy the Pennethorne block and wings along the east and west sides of the Great Court, but the prospect is for a further retraction of civil service activities. King's College, in particular, is looking for expansion space as part of a development plan by Inskip & Jenkins. It took the determination of François Mitterand to banish the French foreign ministry from the Louvre: who has the clout to clear the tax inspectors out of Somerset House?

Above and opposite
The terrace café and the choreographed fountains in the Great Court are among the most striking interventions in this historic ensemble.

SOUTHWARK UNDERGROUND STATION
THE CUT, SE1

MacCORMAC JAMIESON PRICHARD, 1990–2000

The new Southwark station, incorporating a connection between the Jubilee line extension and suburban rail services at Waterloo East (previously a very badly connected, though heavily used, facility), produced what seemed initially a surprising commission. Richard MacCormac's approach to architecture, strongly contextual and rooted in history, is far removed from that of, say, Norman Foster, Ian Ritchie or Wilkinson Eyre, with none of the explicit concern for structural expression that tends to characterize their work. Nonetheless, the station is one of the delights of the Jubilee line extension and one of MacCormac's finest works to date.

It is no coincidence that this is the station serving Tate Modern, as its union of engineering and art is both subtle and appropriate. Like many earlier stations on the Underground, Southwark is located on a street corner amidst an established, downbeat urban scene. The exterior of the ticket hall is dignified, but unshowy, designed as the base of a forthcoming commercial development. The booking hall itself is a drum, relatively compressed in feel and evoking, consciously perhaps, Holden's Arnos Grove of the 1930s. The route from here to the platforms is, in MacCormac's vision, an "episodic journey". The passenger descends escalators to an intermediate concourse, a clearly subterranean space, but lofty in scale –

16 metres high – and filled with natural light from above. On one side, a heavy masonry wall contains the great 'scoops' of the escalator shafts down to the platforms. Balancing it is a curved wall made of 660 pieces of specially cut blue glass, a collaboration between MacCormac, engineers Tony Hunt and Adams Kara Taylor, and artist Alexander Beleschenko – the inspiration, it seems, was Schinkel's famous design for the Queen of the Night's castle in *The Magic Flute*. After the openness of this space, the escalator shafts are compressed, like those in a Holden station, leading to a lower concourse, a barrel-vaulted space lined in unpolished stainless steel from which the platform tunnels are entered.

The engineering challenge at Southwark was considerable, since the station sits under the Victorian viaduct of the railway into Charing Cross. An access tunnel from the intermediate concourse runs through to a new Waterloo East ticket hall, executed as a steel and glass shell wrapped around the viaduct. Not the least achievement of the Jubilee line extension project has been the closer integration of London's transport systems. Given the pace of development in the Bankside and Waterloo areas, the station is a vital new amenity; it seems amazing that it was once seriously proposed to delete it from the Jubilee line extension programme.

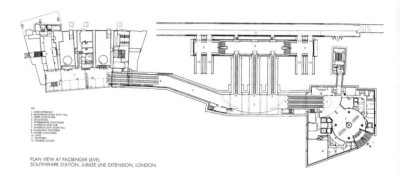

PLAN VIEW AT PASSENGER LEVEL
SOUTHWARK STATION, JUBILEE LINE EXTENSION, LONDON

Above
Plan showing the progression of spaces from the ticket hall, through the upper concourse, to the new Waterloo East concourse.

Opposite, top left
At platform level the new Jubilee line stations reveal a unified aesthetic.

Opposite, top right
Intermediate concourse, showing the curved wall of blue glass.

Opposite, bottom
The vaulted space of the platform-level concourse is pierced by the dramatic staircase.

STRATFORD REGIONAL STATION, E15
WILKINSON EYRE/TROUGHTON McASLAN, 1994–99

Stratford, the 'capital of the East End', is the end of the line for the Jubilee line extension. It has always been an important railway centre: the line from East Anglia into London passed through in the 1840s and a major railway works was developed there. Since the Second World War, the Central line has provided a link to the heart of London. A more recent arrival has been the Docklands Light Railway. The Cross Channel Rail Link, with Stratford a stop on the route from the Channel to St Pancras, will complete this concentration of rail links.

The new station at Stratford had to be far more than an Underground station. The opportunity was taken to improve and rationalize greatly the existing station, where mainline, Underground and North London line services and bus links were badly connected. Wilkinson Eyre created a two-level terminal, with the North London line services integrated into the building, which forms the public face to the entire transport complex. Jubilee line extension services

use surface platforms, with attached staff accommodation in rigorously rational style, designed by Troughton McAslan.

Wilkinson Eyre's great glazed concourse, with a sheer glass façade addressing the town centre, is a virtuoso exercise in terms of its structural economy, thanks to engineers Ove Arup, and innovative use of glazing. The south-facing street front is angled to avoid solar gain and glare. The double skin of the roof is designed to act as a thermal generator, drawing warm air out of the building. The building, which looks like a high-profile air terminal, works wonders for the battered image of public transport.

Wilkinson Eyre was also responsible for the Jubilee line extension's servicing depot at Stratford, designed and built in 1991–96. With all the grandeur of a Victorian train shed, the depot is the operational and spiritual heart of the Jubilee line extension. Sadly, it is completely inaccessible to the public.

Right
The station, with its elegantly sweeping form, serves as a transport hub for the East End and a focal point for Stratford town centre.

Opposite
The lofty hall of the station contrasts with the functional rigour of the new Jubilee line platforms.

THAMES BARRIER PARK
NORTH WOOLWICH ROAD, E16
PATEL TAYLOR ARCHITECTS/GROUP SIGNES/
OVE ARUP & PARTNERS, 1995–2000

The Thames Barrier, 520 metres in width and opened in 1982, could be reckoned the GLC's greatest gift to London as rising tides pose an increasing threat to wide swathes of the capital. The idea of a really large public park – half the size of St James's Park – adjacent to the northern end of the Barrier, on derelict land heavily polluted by industry, was one of the last projects of the London Docklands Development Corporation and was intended as a contribution to the regeneration of the Silvertown area and the Royal Docks. A design competition that elicited over 200 entries was held in 1995, and two schemes, this one and a rival proposal by Kathryn Gustafson/Peter Clash, were shortlisted. The Patel Taylor scheme was implemented in 1997–2000.

The competition brief had referred to "the metropolitan promise of the site as well as the recreational needs of the local population". This was to be a space for all London, not just for East Enders. It was

Patel Taylor's response that won them the job. They proposed a park of five distinct areas or "settings": the Plateau, with its views over the river; the Green Dock, a cutting through this space heavily planted and crossed by bridges, a quiet place for thinking and relaxing; the River Promenade; the Peripheries, with tracks for walkers, runners and cyclists; and a series of play areas set aside for team games and for children. The design of the park is thoroughly architectural, with a strong and legible plan, and its realization in tough and appropriate materials is entirely in keeping with the character of Docklands.

The park is an excellent amenity in its own right, and it was ironic that Ken Livingstone, former leader of the GLC and newly elected Mayor of London, came to open it late in 2000. It has also generated a great deal of development in the surrounding area, with scrapyards and oil depots giving way to houses, schools and shops.

Opposite and above
The park is heavily architectural and provides a variety of spaces, including a memorial, opposite, top right, to the East Enders who were killed in the Second World War.

Key

1 Ticket Hall level
2 District and Circle Line
3 Main Interchange level
4 Jubilee Line Eastbound level
5 Jubilee Line Westbound level
6 Escalators from District and Circle line
  to Main Interchange level
7 Plant
8 Escalators
9 Diaphram Wall
10 New Parliamentary Building

WESTMINSTER UNDERGROUND STATION, SW1

MICHAEL HOPKINS & PARTNERS, 1991–2000

At first sight, the monumentally austere interior of Westminster station, completely rebuilt as part of the Jubilee line extension project, might appear to have little in common with Michael Hopkins's beautifully crafted Portcullis House (see pp. 230–31), of which it forms a vast undercroft. Yet the two projects were designed and built in tandem and are structurally indivisible.

An interchange with the District line at Westminster was planned for the extension project from the beginning. The existing station was part of London's first underground railway, opened in the 1860s, and had to be accommodated (and kept open) as the 40-metre-deep box for the extension was excavated around it. The proximity of Big Ben – a street's width away from one of the biggest holes in London – further complicated the engineering of the station.

Lowering the level of the District line tracks by 300 millimetres – no mean operation in itself – secured headroom for a new booking hall a level below the central courtyard of Portcullis House. The District line is one level below. The Jubilee line extension is accessed via banks of escalators (seventeen in total) threading through the main structural columns, with the deep platforms stacked one above the other outside the edge of the station box.

The predominant impression of the station is one of constant movement. Trimmings are kept to a minimum: the aesthetic is formed by the raw materials of the structure: rough and polished concrete, and stainless steel. Architecture and engineering come together in a fine balance, fulfilling an ambition that lay at the very centre of the Jubilee line extension project.

Opposite
The banks of escalators set amid the steel-and-concrete structure of the deep station activate one of the most exciting spaces on the new Jubilee line.

Left
East–west section, demonstrating how the station provides the structure of Portcullis House above.

District and Circle line platforms, which had to be accommodated between the Jubilee line platforms below and Portcullis House above.

Jubilee line platform, with its distinctive steel panels and the glazed safety screen that is common throughout the Jubilee line extension.

WORLD SQUARES FOR ALL

FOSTER AND PARTNERS, 1997–

The idea of rescuing key areas of central London from domination by road traffic and creating pedestrian-friendly spaces was strongly promoted by Richard Rogers in his 'London as it could be' project of 1986 and in his subsequent campaigns. It was ironic, therefore, that it was Norman Foster, rather than Rogers, who was selected in 1997 to bring the vision to a degree of reality. Promoted by Westminster Council in conjunction with central government, World Squares for All focused on both Trafalgar Square and Parliament Square, both of which feature public spaces islanded by busy roads. Foster's radical proposals proved controversial, since it was suggested that curbing traffic in these locations would create traffic jams elsewhere and damage the commercial life of the capital. Tourism is, in fact, one of the major generators of wealth and employment in the West End, and the project addressed the setting of such key monuments as the National Gallery, Westminster Abbey and the Palace of Westminster. Westminster Council, however, steadily backtracked on its commitment to the project, which seemed to drift into limbo.

A major boost to World Squares for All came with the election of Ken Livingstone as London mayor in 2000. This provided the impetus for the Foster scheme to start on the Trafalgar Square remodelling. The road that separated the square from the National Gallery has been removed and pedestrians are finally allowed to flow freely between the two.

Foster has now been commissioned to undertake the pedestrianization of Parliament Square, and the Sunday closure of the Victoria Embankment to motor traffic is also being considered.

Opposite, top and bottom
The closure to traffic of the north side of Trafalgar Square has provided a grand promenade linking the National Gallery to St Martin's in the Fields and Nelson's Column.

Below
The square has become a lively focus for entertainments and public meetings (left). The refurbishment allowed for the construction of new visitor facilities such as cafés and WCs (right).

DARWIN CENTRE, THE NATURAL HISTORY MUSEUM SOUTH KENSINGTON, SW7

HOK INTERNATIONAL, 1992–2002

HOK's Darwin Centre, which opened in autumn 2002, is the latest addition to London's densely developed museum and education quarter of South Kensington. The building stands west of Alfred Waterhouse's Grade I-listed Natural History Museum, the Science Museum's Wellcome Wing (by MacCormac Jamieson Prichard) is a close neighbour, and Imperial College's packed campus lies just to the north. The HOK building is, in fact, the first phase of the Darwin Centre. Phase Two, won in competition by Danish practice C.F. Møller Architects, is scheduled for completion by 2007, replacing a very utilitarian inter-war laboratory block.

The Darwin Centre project reflects The Natural History Museum's role as a place of research – it employs 350 scientists – as well as an educational and visitor facility. Its Spirit Collection contains up to 22,000,000 zoological specimens preserved in alcohol and gathered over the last 200 years; some were brought from Australia by Captain Cook in 1768. The collection was previously housed in extremely inadequate premises, which were inaccessible to the public.

The 12,000-square-metre, £21,000,000 centre reflects the museum's aim to open up the collections more widely to the public and to foster interest in its research work.

It combines three functions: a store for the specimens, laboratories for researchers and controlled access for visitors (up to fourteen guided tours are run daily). The building is divided into three zones reflecting its mixture of roles. To the north is an eight-storey climate-controlled store. The south side of the centre contains laboratories and offices; visitors can see scientists at work from the connecting walkways along the side of the central atrium, which forms the heart of the building.

HOK's architecture is well judged in its relationship to Waterhouse's masterpiece. The centre is clearly subsidiary to the main museum building, and has a tough, almost industrial quality: internal finishes are far from extravagant. A visual connection to Waterhouse, however, is provided by the use of terracotta panels to frame the fully glazed southern façade. Supported on specially cast brackets (deliberately zoomorphic in appearance), the outer façade is a *tour de force* in itself. Behind it, the inner skin of the building is screened by sun-tracking louvres that close down when the sun strikes directly on the south front. The roof is formed partly of ETFE (ethyltetrafluoroethylene) panels, which provide effective insulation while allowing daylight to penetrate the atrium.

DULWICH PICTURE GALLERY, SE21
RICK MATHER ARCHITECTS, 1996–2000

For John Summerson, Dulwich Picture Gallery was not only "one of [Sir John] Soane's most able and revealing designs", but also a building that "as a whole reaches a level of emotional eloquence and technical performance rare in English, or indeed in European architecture". The gallery was constructed in 1811–14 under the terms of the will of the late Sir Francis Bourgeois (1757–1811), to house his remains and those of the great collector Noel Desenfans, who had died a few years earlier, leaving a collection of 370 pictures that went to Dulwich. The combination of mausoleum and art gallery was uncommon, the site, hard against the old buildings of Dulwich College to the north, awkward: Soane envisaged the building as one side of a quadrangle, but this was never realized. There were several minor extensions, and a certain amount of internal rearrangement, during the first half of the twentieth century. During the Second World War, the gallery was severely damaged by bombing in 1940 and 1944 and was rebuilt, to a tight budget, in 1950–52.

By the 1970s the gallery was a rather forlorn place, with serious funding problems and still run by the college. Giles Waterfield's directorship saw major changes: independent trustees took over, the building was made more attractive, with Soanean colours partly restored inside, and visitor numbers doubled; the educational activities of the gallery, in particular, blossomed. Rick Mather's millennium project, combining refurbishment and restoration of Soane's hugely admired and widely emulated gallery and the construction of a major extension to provide storage, offices and visitor and custom-made education facilities, was the culmination of this process of recovery and is the most successful of Mather's three major London museum projects of this period.

Any addition to an iconic monument of this order was bound to be controversial. An ideas competition of the early 1990s – there was no funding – proposed an extension to the south of Soane's building. Mather was the winner of a limited competition in 1996. The success of his scheme, funded by Lottery money and private donations, lies in its lightness of touch and its emphasis on redefining the important garden setting of the gallery and connecting it to the village street beyond. The new development provides a cloister that links the Old College with the gallery and provides space for new and relocated activities, freeing up Soane's interiors for the display of works of art. The gallery itself was carefully restored, with original decorative schemes and finishes reinstated and new environmental and security systems installed.

Above
The original galleries by Sir John Soane have been conscientiously refurbished.

Opposite
The new cloister links the existing buildings, and provides office and education spaces and a café.

HORNIMAN MUSEUM EXTENSION
FOREST HILL, SE23

ALLIES & MORRISON, 1995–2002

The Horniman, tucked away in the south London suburb of Forest Hill, is one of the most idiosyncratic of the capital's smaller museums in terms of both its architecture and its contents (a mix of ethnography, stuffed animals and musical instruments). It is a well-loved local institution, established for "the recreation, instruction and enjoyment" of south Londoners, but it is not on the tourist trail. Its original building, however, opened in 1901, is a remarkable and – for Britain – unusual example of the Art Nouveau style, designed by Charles Harrison Townsend for philanthropist founder Frederick Horniman.

The museum stands next to a public park, also created by Horniman, but until the completion of the Allies & Morrison scheme it turned its back to the park, with an entrance only from the busy London Road. Allies & Morrison was commissioned to develop expansion plans in 1995. The brief was to provide a new gallery for temporary exhibitions, an education centre, café and shop. Issues of accessibility had to be addressed as part of a major development programme that also saw the repair and refurbishment of the original building. The decision was taken to reorientate the museum so that the main entrance is now from the park.

Allies & Morrison's extension, stone-fronted and with a metal-clad curved roof, takes its form and scale from Townsend's original: to the gardens, for example, it is faced in red brick. Inside, a daylit, double-height space provides access to all parts of the building. The café, shop and education rooms are at ground level, with the new galleries, including a space specially designed for displaying musical instruments, below (actually at street level, since the slope on the site is quite dramatic). To the north, the building opens up to a paved court, where a restored Victorian conservatory provides a venue for social events, and to the park beyond.

This is a finely crafted, highly sensitive scheme that integrates old and new painlessly and brings light and air to the mysterious world of the Horniman. Not that the character of the original has been diluted: it is still possible to use Townsend's entrance, up steps from the street. The amenities of the museum, which is a real community asset, have been vastly improved and a Victorian institution given a new lease of life.

Above
Allies & Morrison's carefully considered extension takes its cue in terms of scale and materials from Townsend's original building of 1901.

Opposite
The extension is arranged around a double-height space from which café, shop, education spaces and new galleries can be accessed.

MUSEUM OF FASHION AND TEXTILES
BERMONDSEY STREET, SE1

RICARDO LEGORRETA/ALAN CAMP ARCHITECTS, 1995–2003

This is Ricardo Legorreta's only European project so far, though he is currently working on a hotel in Bilbao. The idea of commissioning the Mexican master was fashion designer Zandra Rhodes's – he had built a house for a friend of hers in California. Surprisingly, perhaps, Southwark planners and the local community liked his ideas and welcomed Rhodes's vision of creating a personal museum for her collection – like Paxton Locher's Jerwood Space in nearby Union Street it is a spin-off

of the process of arts-based regeneration spreading out from Tate Modern. Not even the bright colours dimmed their enthusiasm and, after years of planning, work began, with local practice Alan Camp Architects collaborating with Legorreta. One part of Camp's task was to make the scheme commercially viable, and eight apartments were included, as well as a restaurant (Rhodes has the penthouse).

The vivid colours applied to the development are typical of Legorreta but

not of London; the combination of shocking pink with vivid orange is the antithesis of conventional 'good' taste. In the 1980s Postmodernists tried to achieve equally striking results but rarely, with the possible exception of Piers Gough, hit the right note. This development could be on the edge of downtown Los Angeles but looks good right where it is.

Below and opposite
The museum, with apartments above, forms an exotic addition to an otherwise gritty urban landscape.

NATIONAL MARITIME MUSEUM GREENWICH, SE10

RICK MATHER ARCHITECTS/BUILDING
DESIGN PARTNERSHIP, 1996–99

Rick Mather was brought into the National Maritime Museum project after a previous development project had been rejected for Lottery funding. The museum was established at Greenwich in the 1930s, inhabiting the long nineteenth-century wings built either side of Inigo Jones's famous Queen's House to contain the Royal Naval Asylum, a school for seamen's orphans. The result was a museum that extended in a straight line, east to west, with few really impressive spaces.

Mather took up the (fairly obvious) idea – part of the abandoned scheme – to roof over an open court, which had been merely wasted space in the western wing of the museum, and use it to contain large exhibits. But his new masterplan was effectively a reappraisal of the entire building, concentrating on establishing new connections between disparate spaces. The most spectacular element in the scheme is the reconstructed Neptune Court, with what is claimed to be Europe's largest free-span glazed roof, designed with the assistance of Building Design Partnership (BDP) engineers. The roof covers a two-level public space: a raised square occupies the centre, with enclosed galleries, used for displaying light-sensitive materials, below. There are bridge links from this level to the first-floor museum galleries. The strategy ensures optimum use of space, but the visual impact of the glazed roof is inevitably reduced.

Mather's role at Greenwich has since expanded: he has designed a visitor centre, and is developing a masterplan, for the Royal Naval Hospital, now run by an independent trust and used for educational and cultural purposes.

Opposite and below
The central court, with its glazed roof and walls either side of the existing stone pavilion, adds a new dimension to the previously linear spaces of the museum.

NATIONAL PORTRAIT GALLERY EXTENSION (ONDAATJE WING), ST MARTIN'S PLACE, WC2

JEREMY DIXON.EDWARD JONES, 1994–2000

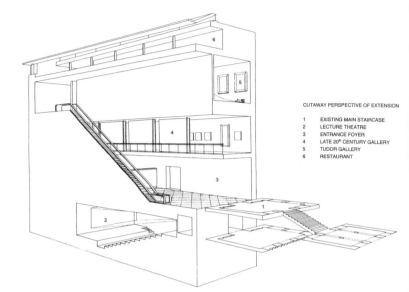

CUTAWAY PERSPECTIVE OF EXTENSION

1 EXISTING MAIN STAIRCASE
2 LECTURE THEATRE
3 ENTRANCE FOYER
4 LATE 20th CENTURY GALLERY
5 TUDOR GALLERY
6 RESTAURANT

Jeremy Dixon and Edward Jones, who formed their present partnership in 1989, have been identified in the past as Postmodernists: the Royal Opera House, on which Dixon began work as early as 1984, is essentially an urban collage. In contrast, the National Portrait Gallery millennium project is an exercise in minimalism, an ingenious and economical insertion into the tight fabric of the West End that has transformed the character of the gallery.

The original National Portrait Gallery building dates from 1896 and is the work of the church architect Ewan Christian, who squeezed it on to an awkward site behind the National Gallery (to which it appeared to form an addition). The interior suffered from its unavoidably vertical character – the Duveen Wing of the 1930s utilized the only space available for expansion. Many visitors never got as far as the top floor. Some – Ian Nairn, for example – loved the melancholy quiet of the place, but many Londoners never ventured inside. Dixon.Jones, appointed by the director at the time, Charles Saumarez Smith and his trustees in 1994, broke the impasse in which the gallery was caught, proposing that a rear service yard, overlooked by National Gallery offices, be developed as a new central circulation space. In return for losing its rights of light, the National Gallery was ceded National Portrait Gallery space along St Martin's Place. The new wing is slotted into the yard. A three-storey-high atrium contains an escalator that invites visitors to ascend to the top of the building and percolate downwards – at every level, the new wing is smoothly linked into the Christian building. (Some nifty adjustments to levels, with steps and mosaic floors seamlessly adapted, were required – there is, for the first time, total access for the disabled.) The structure is extremely economical – new twentieth-century galleries at first-floor level are suspended from above. A lecture theatre is provided at basement level.

The finishing touch to the transformation is provided by the new restaurant, a loggia that perches on top of the extension. It looks out across the domes, chimneys and skylights of William Wilkins's National Gallery – a miniature Classical landscape – to Nelson's Column, Whitehall and the Palace of Westminster. There was much agonizing over its design – planners feared it could intrude into views of the National Gallery. But its presence is elusive. Indeed, that term could be applied to the entire scheme: nothing seems to have changed at the National Portrait Gallery, until you get past the front door. The charm of the place has not been lost, but it has been intelligently equipped to deal with the demands of a new generation of visitors.

Top right
The extension is shoehorned into a former service yard of the gallery.

Bottom right and opposite
The new wing, with its prominent three-storey escalator, links all levels of the nineteenth-century building, many of which were previously little visited.

THE QUEEN ELIZABETH II GREAT COURT
THE BRITISH MUSEUM, WC1
FOSTER AND PARTNERS, 1994–2003

Opposite
The Great Court has been conceived as a major public space, utilizing areas of the museum previously inaccessible to the general public.

Below
Long section, showing how the Great Court forms part of a continuous route through the building.

The most prestigious of the many London projects on which Norman Foster was engaged at the turn of the century, the Great Court starts with the basically simple idea of turning an underused open courtyard into a glazed covered space, a central social and circulation focus for the museum; Rick Mather's revamps of the Wallace Collection and, with Building Design Partnership (BDP) engineers, National Maritime Museum are variations on this theme. Modern structural engineering and glazing technology facilitates the operation, providing an economy of means that the Victorians (who invented the idea of the winter garden) lacked.

Where the Great Court scores above both these projects, however, is the fact that it is located in central London, at the heart of one of the most famous – and most visited, and frequently overcrowded – cultural institutions in the world. It was conceived not just as an addition to the amenities of the British Museum but equally as a new public space for London, open late into the evening, a space where you can linger but that also forms the most convenient through route from the London University precinct to Great Russell Street. The huge mass of the museum has become permeable, part of the fabric of the city. For some, the monumental gravitas and the cool – even icy – aesthetic of the space are a deterrent to relaxing in the café areas – which admittedly seem incidental and somewhat transient, crushed by the grandeur of their surroundings – but the numbers of visitors thronging the Great Court on a typical day make the scheme seem inevitable, the only way in which the museum could sensibly develop for the future.

The British Museum was built in 1823–47 to Greek Revival designs by Sir Robert Smirke. The entilade of galleries was arranged around the central court, "a dull, miserable looking space" as a contemporary critic described it. In 1854–55 Smirke's brother Sydney constructed the famous Round Reading Room in the middle of the court. Over the next century, all the space around the drum of the Reading Room was filled with bookstacks: the central court became a distant memory. The decision to remove the British Library to a new building at St Pancras – it opened in 1998 – freed up the space around the Reading Room (which itself had to be retained) for museum use. Foster was the winner of a competition held in 1994. Work started on site in spring 1998, and was completed in two and a half years – a considerable achievement in itself.

As part of the project, the much-damaged façades of the court were extensively repaired, and the demolished south portico rebuilt in replica. Foster, in collaboration with engineers Buro Happold, designed the lightweight roof structure with 3312 glass panels, each one a different size owing to the slightly off-centre placement of the Reading Room in the court. Its structure rests on the perimeter walls and on slender columns buried beneath the new cladding of the drum. The roof provides a calm, even light, regardless of external conditions, and its airy elegance contrasts with the solidity of the great staircases wrapped around the Reading Room, now a public reference library, its original décor carefully reinstated. Education facilities and lecture rooms are buried beneath the floor of the Great Court. A separate, but related, Foster project, has located new ethnography galleries north of the space, finally breaking down the barrier to circulation imposed by Sir John Burnet's Edward VII Galleries of 1914.

Allowing visitors to 'read' the museum and its extraordinary collections in a new way – traditionally it was a wearying procession of didactic spaces – the Great Court begs comparison with I.M. Pei's ambitious reworking of the Louvre as an exercise in the modernization not only of museum spaces but also of the relationship between the museum and the urban community.

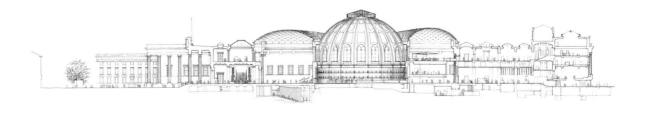

TATE BRITAIN, MILLBANK, SW1
JOHN MILLER & PARTNERS, 1990–2001

John Miller & Partners is one of Britain's most accomplished museum and gallery design practices: it completed a refurbishment of the Serpentine Gallery in 1997 and, more recently, major schemes at the National Gallery of Scotland, Edinburgh, and the Fitzwilliam Museum, Cambridge. The practice's involvement with the Tate began a decade ago with a masterplan for the future development of what was the Tate Gallery, Millbank, and is now, thanks to its director, Nicholas Serota, Tate Britain.

Twentieth-century additions to the original Tate (a dull affair in composite Classical manner, opened in 1897) include, most strikingly, James Stirling's Clore Gallery (1987). Earlier accretions include John Russell Pope's handsome Duveen Gallery and the range of galleries added in the north-eastern corner of the complex by R. Llewellyn-Davies and the Public Services Agency (PSA) in the 1970s. In the early 1980s Jeremy Dixon designed a new basement café (subsequently dismantled). John Miller was responsible for the more recent bookshop and the overhaul of various gallery spaces.

Miller's major Lottery-funded refit of Tate Britain, opened in autumn 2001, provides nine new galleries, three on the main level and six more at basement level, plus a new bookshop, IT room and entrance foyer on Atterbury Street – a natural point of entry for the large numbers of visitors who arrive at the Tate from Pimlico Tube station and completely accessible to the disabled. (The external landscaping associated with the scheme, including an entrance ramp, has been designed by Allies & Morrison.) Perhaps most significantly, a new triple-height staircase hall now provides a convenient connection between the two levels. The basement (or rather undercroft, since the main level is a *piano nobile*) formerly contained a limited number of galleries (it was easy to overlook them) plus the restaurant, café, cloakrooms and various storage and administrative spaces. An open court behind the Duveen Gallery provided another obvious space for expansion. The galleries incorporate sophisticated natural and artificial lighting systems, with a system of louvres and solar baffles to control solar gain.

The Tate Britain project represents a vigorous response to the perceived problem – not one that occurs to those who like to see art in comfort – of falling visitor numbers at Millbank (the 'Tate Modern effect'). It makes Tate Britain a more convenient and enjoyable place to visit and addresses the specific needs of important groups of visitors. Yet the best way of bringing back the visitors may be better exhibitions and a reconsidered hanging policy. Tate Britain will never have the spectacular effect of its sister institution at Bankside, but it contains just as many masterpieces and now possesses the spaces to show them to best effect.

Opposite and top
The new staircase is the most important feature of the project, providing a convenient link between the two main levels of the gallery.

Above
Nine new galleries have been provided as part of the new scheme.

TATE MODERN, BANKSIDE, SE1

HERZOG & DE MEURON, 1994–2000

The Tate Gallery of Modern Art – subsequently Tate Modern – has been the outstanding success among all the projects generated nationwide by the National Lottery. As other attractions tightened their belts or even closed their doors, Tate Modern boomed – two million people visited during the first three months of opening and the hordes continue to pour in. The (already glittering) career of Sir Nicholas Serota received another boost, as did the ongoing process of regeneration in Southwark. It has helped that admission (except for special exhibitions) is free, and that the new Tate is in London, just across the Thames from St Paul's, and close to a newly opened station on the Jubilee line extension. But the building, like Paris's Pompidou Centre in the 1980s, has become a massive attraction in its own right – ironically enough, since it had been universally condemned when first built. There were those, moreover, who saw the decision to locate Tate Modern in a converted building, rather than a new landmark design, as a cop-out.

The idea of Tate Modern (controversial in itself) was Nicholas Serota's, and a number of potential sites for a new building were considered. The decision to develop the redundant Bankside power station as a container for the new museum was a matter of common sense. Bankside had been closed for thirteen years (though a massive sub-station along the southern edge of the building remains in use). It was not listed, but Sir Giles Scott's monumental temple of power (completed as recently as 1963) had its admirers. More to the point, it offered all the space the Tate needed, with ample scope for later expansion, and conversion was cheaper than building something new.

An architectural competition was launched in 1994, with the entries whittled down to a shortlist first of thirteen, then of six – Rafael Moneo, Tadao Ando, Renzo Piano, Rem Koolhaas, David Chipperfield and Herzog & de Meuron. Winning Tate Modern catapulted the relatively little-known (at least in Britain) Swiss practice into the front ranks – in 2001, it won the coveted Pritzker Prize.

For the admirers of Scott's building, the winning proposal had its attractions: the external envelope of the power station was to remain largely intact (some competitors had proposed to demolish the prominent chimney and to make radical additions to the exterior). Inside, the vast turbine hall was to be retained as a public forum, entered via a huge ramp from the west, with the galleries and other new spaces inserted into the flanking boiler house.

Tate Modern opened in May 2000 amid massive – generally positive – publicity, with the turbine hall filled with an exhibition of large-scale works by the veteran sculptor Louise Bourgeois. A few years into its life, the strengths and weaknesses of Herzog & de Meuron's scheme have steadily emerged. The turbine hall itself is a genuinely popular space that has hosted some spectacular installations. In contrast, the galleries seem too small for the numbers of visitors they attract and lacking in flexibility, while the lifts and escalators are hard pressed to cope with the crowds. The so-called 'grand staircase' – introduced

as an afterthought and rather coarsely detailed – is neither grand nor very helpful as a means of access to the upper floors. The top-floor restaurant is equally inadequate in scale. Herzog & de Meuron's 'light beam', of which the restaurant forms a part, is effectively a corridor, with only partial views across the river to the City. (The best views are obtained from the Tate Friends' room, a level below.) The awkward illuminated cap added to Scott's massive chimney at a late stage in the project is not an adornment: the plan to create a viewing gallery at the top of the stack has not so far been realized.

Yet the defects of the project are outweighed by its sheer bravado and its sophisticated and confident approach to the recycling of an industrial monument, which could easily have vanished (and would have been missed). Moreover, with large areas of the building available for conversion in the future, Tate Modern is an ongoing project of heroic ambition. It has changed the cultural face of London.

Above
The crimson interior of the auditorium contrasts with the subdued hues of the rest of the museum.

Opposite
Overlooking the River Thames in Southwark, the building's original turbine hall has been retained, though transformed into a vast public space, while the galleries and ancillary facilities are grouped over seven levels on the north side, accessed by prominent escalators and a discreet staircase.

THE WALLACE COLLECTION MANCHESTER SQUARE, W1

RICK MATHER ARCHITECTS, 1996–2000

The Wallace Collection has an exotic history. It was assembled by four successive marquises of Hertford and left by the Francophile 4th marquis, an eccentric recluse, to his illegitimate son, Sir Richard Wallace, who moved it from Paris to London and installed it in Hertford House. It opened to the public in 1900 and was, at least until recently, one of the least-known major collections in London. The conditions that only the core collection could be shown in the house and that nothing could be loaned for display elsewhere may have blinded Londoners to its enormous quality.

Rick Mather's task – he won the job in a limited competition – was comprehensively to re-equip the Wallace in time for its centenary, addressing issues of security, conservation, access, education and storage; he was also to allow more of the collection to be shown and provide the café and shop that museum visitors now demand, plus a lecture theatre. The site was completely blocked by adjacent developments, making any horizontal extension impossible. The solution was to capitalize on all the underused space within the building, including the rear wing, the basement level and the open court that formed the centre of the mansion. The adaptation of the basement and its connection to the ground floor of the building are skilfully managed – there is now a lecture theatre and a well-equipped education centre.

The typical Victorian museum was understood as a didactic experience, in which the visitor was content to shuffle from room to room, taking in the displays in a prescribed manner. People are no longer so compliant. As at the British Museum Great Court, the glazing-over of the central space at the Wallace Collection allows visitors to break out of the procession of rooms and even to take a coffee or lunch break. On this occasion, the roof does not have the sense of lightness and exhilaration that Mather showed at Dulwich, nor is the space large enough to provide a convincing new dimension to the building. But it has proved attractive enough to pull in local office workers, who have discovered the Wallace as a calm retreat from the tumult of the West End.

Opposite
The redevelopment has not only enclosed a former garden, making it the architectural focus of the museum, but has also opened up former basement levels as galleries and ancillary spaces.

Left
The central court, surmounted by a glazed roof, incorporates a restaurant and access to perimeter galleries.

WELLCOME WING, THE SCIENCE MUSEUM EXHIBITION ROAD, SW7

MacCORMAC JAMIESON PRICHARD, 1996–2000

Big, bold and blue, Richard MacCormac's Wellcome Wing is a highly efficient, stylish container for a wide range of exhibits and activities that exploits to the full the available space on the Science Museum's cramped site in South Kensington. Not many years ago, MacCormac was best known for his college buildings in Oxford and Cambridge, projects that drew on his strong sense of history, with results that were always interesting but occasionally over-elaborate in their referentiality. Generous budgets, perhaps, might explain this tendency.

The 11,000-square-metre Wellcome Wing, built to a design-and-build contract for just over £21,000,000, is something very different and, together with the superb Southwark Jubilee line station, reflects MacCormac Jamieson Prichard's strong emergence as London architects – the practice's appointment in 2001 as

architects for the redevelopment of the BBC's Broadcasting House site was a further triumph.

The dominant idea behind the Wellcome Wing is flexibility and adaptability – the shape of the building reflects the dynamic nature of the museum's subject-matter. The wing forms an extension westwards of the existing buildings and a further addition, a new conference centre, terminates the development to the west. An IMAX cinema was one of the facilities to be housed and is conceived as a volume hanging within the space – its sloping auditorium floor is read as a dramatic ceiling, sweeping up to reveal open galleries on three levels. Construction is tough and simple: concrete columns with steel trusses and steel grilles used extensively as cladding. A huge double-glazed blue-glass window at the west end of the wing fills the interior with a rich but suffused light.

Right
The rich colouring of the Wellcome Wing's interior masks a straightforward rational plan.

Opposite
The ceiling, seen here, is formed by the underside of a new auditorium that helps to create a visually exciting space.

who am I?

1

2

digitopolis

3

infuture

launch pad

↓

LEISURE

BATTERSEA POWER STATION
SIR PHILIP DOWSON/ARUP ASSOCIATES/NICHOLAS GRIMSHAW & PARTNERS/
BENOY/BENSON & FORSYTH

BRITISH AIRWAYS LONDON EYE
MARKS BARFIELD ARCHITECTS

GREAT EASTERN HOTEL
THE MANSER PRACTICE

HAMSTEAD THEATRE
BENNETTS ASSOCIATES

IDEA STORE
ADJAYE ASSOCIATES

THE KING'S LIBRARY, BRITISH MUSEUM
HOK INTERNATIONAL

LABAN DANCE CENTRE
HERZOG & DE MEURON

LONDON REGATTA CENTRE
IAN RITCHIE ARCHITECTS

MEDIA CENTRE, LORD'S CRICKET GROUND
FUTURE SYSTEMS

PECKHAM LIBRARY
ALSOP ARCHITECTS

THE PLACE
ALLIES & MORRISON

THE ROUNDHOUSE
JOHN McASLAN + PARTNERS

ROYAL COURT THEATRE
HAWORTH TOMPKINS ARCHITECTS

ROYAL FESTIVAL HALL REFURBISHMENT
ALLIES & MORRISON

ROYAL OPERA HOUSE
JEREMY DIXON.EDWARD JONES/BUILDING DESIGN PARTNERSHIP

SADLERS WELLS
ARTS TEAM @ RHWL/NICHOLAS HARE ARCHITECTS

SOHO THEATRE
PAXTON LOCHER ARCHITECTS

THE WOMEN'S LIBRARY
WRIGHT & WRIGHT ARCHITECTS

BATTERSEA POWER STATION, SW8

SIR PHILIP DOWSON/ARUP ASSOCIATES/NICHOLAS GRIMSHAW & PARTNERS/BENOY/BENSON & FORSYTH, 2001–

Battersea Power Station is a building that is both loved and loathed. For those of a functionalist bent, Giles Scott's architectural coating, which "would have made Telford or Rennie throw up", as Ian Nairn commented, is insufferable. Even admirers of Scott's work regard Bankside (now Tate Modern) as finer. Yet there was general relief, nearly twenty years ago, when listing saved the power station from possible demolition. It is hard to imagine this stretch of the Thames without it.

The subsequent failure of an ambitious project to convert the building into a giant (and very controversial) leisure complex left it bereft, with a side elevation demolished and the interior open to the weather. Since the power station was acquired by Parkview International, a succession of architectural practices has worked on proposals for conversion and for the development of the adjacent, very large (fourteen-hectare) site – the key issue is creating a commercially viable scheme that respects the monumental presence of the listed building. The balance is fine.

The advent of Sir Philip Dowson, formerly of Arup Associates, as masterplanning supremo seems to have welded Parkview's proposals into a balanced scheme that satisfies most interests. The most sensitive element, the conversion of the power station itself, has sensibly been allocated to Nicholas Grimshaw & Partners, working with Benoy. Grimshaw's scheme will turn the building into a huge auditorium suitable for a wide range of events, with subsidiary retail and leisure amenities. Grimshaw does not seek to reinstate the fabric lost in the 1980s, but uses the opportunity created to bring natural light and a sense of space into the interior. All significant surviving features, including a remarkable control room, will be retained.

Grimshaw's emphatic vocabulary of metal and glass is appropriately applied to the design of the new riverside jetty, which incorporates existing industrial remnants, including two fine cranes that are a vital element in the riverside scene. The jetty, constructed on an existing concrete base, is designed to serve a new riverboat service – reflecting a welcome emphasis on public transport – as well as serving as a twenty-first-century version of the Victorian pleasure pier. An ingenious 'see-saw' arrangement is proposed to allow boats to load and unload passengers from 150-seat glazed pods simultaneously.

Above
The new riverside jetty will provide access to a new riverboat service carrying visitors to and from the site.

Right
The reconstruction of lost elements of the building will be executed in a lightweight glazed manner, in contrast to Giles Scott's monumental brickwork.

BRITISH AIRWAYS LONDON EYE
SOUTH BANK, SE1

MARKS BARFIELD ARCHITECTS, 1993–2000

The idea of the London Eye, perhaps the most popular of all London's millennium projects, emerged late in 1993 when David Marks and Julia Barfield produced proposals for a giant wheel in response to an ideas competition launched by a Sunday newspaper. During 1994 the idea turned into a feasible project as the architects worked on the scheme with engineer Jane Wernick of Arup Associates, forming their own company to build it. A site was found close to County Hall, across the Thames from the Palace of Westminster. The Millennium Wheel, as it was initially described, was controversial: the chairman of the Royal Fine Art Commission, for example, became a vociferous opponent. Nonetheless, Marks Barfield pressed on, enrolling British Airways as a development partner in 1995. Planning consent was given in October 1996, and the search for

specialist collaborators began. Work began on site in January 1999. The plan was to open on New Year's Eve, just under a year later. By summer, the 335-tonne structure was complete, cantilevered off the South Bank and awaiting the final lift. Subsequent delays in lifting the wheel led to its formal opening being postponed until March 2000.

Spanning 135 metres, the height of the spire of Salisbury Cathedral, and carrying thirty-two capsules (each holding up to twenty-five passengers), the Eye is a large object. Yet its impact on the London skyline – it can be seen from Kensington Gardens – is quite ethereal. Moving at a steady half a mile per hour, it provides staggering views across London from the Thames Estuary to Windsor. Some early criticisms of the project focused on the fact that big wheels were nothing new, as George Ferris had set his 120-metre-high wheel spinning in 1893.

The issue turned out to be irrelevant. It was not so much the originality of the idea or the quality of the technology that mattered – and the London Eye is as far removed from a Ferris wheel as a TGV from Puffing Billy – as the piquancy of the siting. Within six months of its opening the Eye had attracted six million visitors. The idea of having pure fun on the South Bank, forgotten since the closure of the Festival of Britain, and peering down on the homes of the Prime Minister and Queen proved irresistible. The Eye is not quite, as some have claimed, the Eiffel Tower of the twenty-first century. It may not be around in a hundred years (though it is unlikely to be dismantled when its limited planning consent expires), but for the moment it is a London sight that everyone wants to see and experience.

Below and opposite
Despite its monumental scale, the British Airways London Eye has a delicate presence on the London skyline.

GREAT EASTERN HOTEL
LIVERPOOL STREET, EC2
THE MANSER PRACTICE, 1995–2000

The Great Eastern Hotel was described by Sir John Betjeman, lover of all things Victorian, as "the only hotel in the City, and a very good one". The hotel was built, adjacent to Liverpool Street station, in the 1880s and extended by R.W. Edis in 1901. The lack of adequate connections between the two parts of the hotel was always a problem, though the Great Eastern retained its solid reputation into the post-war years. More recently, starved of investment, it declined into a backwater. The Manser Practice's client for the £65,000,000 refurbishment completed in 2000 was a consortium that included design and restaurant magnate Sir Terence Conran. Five new restaurants and bars were included in the reconstruction, which also increased the number of guest rooms by 40%.

The radical upgrading of the listed building included not only the renewal of all services and complete external restoration, but also the total rebuilding of the top two floors, where a new roof structure is punctuated by circular 'bull's eye' *oculi*, designed in the spirit of the Victorians. The reception was relocated eastwards, with a circular lightwell cut into its ceiling and extending to the top of the hotel. The key move in the scheme was, however, the creation of a striking atrium at first-floor level, linking the previously disconnected wings and giving the Great Eastern a new social hub. Many of the bedrooms look down into this space, which contains a carefully detailed lift shaft, clad in perforated metal mesh, to which the main boiler flue, made of polished stainless steel, is attached.

The revived Great Eastern appeals to City tastes – high style combined with a reassuring emphasis on comfort. This is no designer hotel, yet the marriage of an historic institution with modern design sets a lead for the renewal of other big nineteenth-century London hotels.

Opposite and left
The newly constructed atrium, with its striking lift and boiler shafts, now forms the core of the hotel, and is overlooked by a number of the bedrooms.

HAMPSTEAD THEATRE, ETON AVENUE
SWISS COTTAGE, NW3

BENNETTS ASSOCIATES, 1994–2003

The new Hampstead Theatre is the first entirely new theatre built in London since the completion of Denys Lasdun's National Theatre, on the South Bank, in 1975. It provides a well-equipped permanent home for an institution that has built up a striking artistic reputation over nearly forty years despite using distinctly makeshift premises.

By the 1990s the extended Portakabin, next to the Swiss Cottage Baths and Library, that served as Hampstead Theatre was in a poor state. Bennetts Associates was commissioned as early as 1994 to work on plans for a new theatre, initially on the same site, but it soon became clear that there were advantages in relocating it to the north, close to Eton Avenue, where it would replace an unsightly block of public conveniences. Bennetts subsequently produced a masterplan for the entire site, in line with Camden Council's aim to regenerate the area. In the 1960s Basil Spence had proposed a new town hall for Camden at Swiss Cottage, alongside the baths and library, but it was never realized. Much of the site therefore remained unresolved and rather unpleasant left-over open space, shut off from the street. The baths have now been demolished, while the library, a listed building, has been refurbished by John McAslan. New leisure facilities are being developed, together with housing, to a concept by Terry Farrell. The landscape plan for the site has been developed by Gustafson Porter.

The new theatre, finally built in 2000–03 with the aid of Lottery funding, contains a single elliptical auditorium, with flexible seating for up to 330 people, that aims to retain the sense of intimacy that was the great strength of the old theatre while doubling seating capacity. The stage, adaptable for proscenium or open-plan productions, and workshop facilities are vastly improved, as are the dressing-rooms and offices; there is also a dedicated rehearsal space and education room (which can be used as a small studio theatre).

The main entrance is directly from Eton Avenue. Once inside, it becomes apparent to the visitor that the building has three storeys, two above ground and one below. Bridges and ramps channel audiences into the auditorium. Mechanical services are concentrated at basement level in a space that extends below the adjacent landscaped park. The aim was to provide access to the building at street level, removing the need for ramps or lifts. Achieving this meant securing consent from other building owners to move the car-park ramp serving an adjacent office block: it now runs through the theatre basement.

The auditorium reads as a strongly modelled solid mass, clad in matt zinc, clearly rising through the largely transparent pavilion (in which areas of timber slatting punctuate the glazing), which contains the foyers and other public spaces. Finishes in the foyer areas are simple and durable – steel, concrete and timber – with lighting devised by Martin Richman dramatizing the space. The auditorium is lined in timber, with colour adding warmth and texture. The architects cite the rustic Georgian theatre at Richmond, North Yorkshire, as an exemplar for the comfortable but informal ambience they have sought to create.

Bennetts Associates had no experience of theatre design when it tackled this project, and perhaps this was an advantage. The building reflects close collaboration between client and architect. It remains to be seen what impact the move to new premises will have on the famously innovative Hampstead Theatre, but Swiss Cottage has certainly gained an impressive new public landmark.

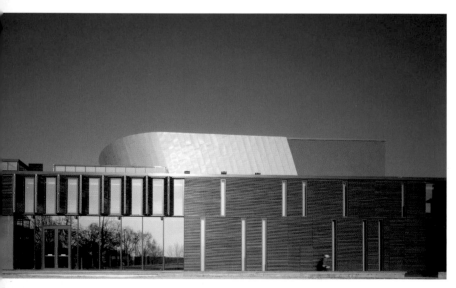

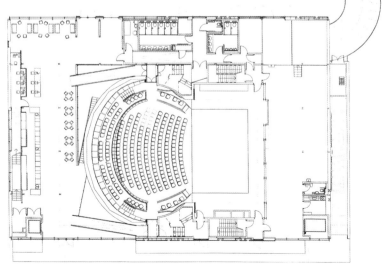

IDEA STORE, WHITECHAPEL, E1

ADJAYE ASSOCIATES, 2001–05

The Idea Store project – actually a public library, designed for Tower Hamlets Council – is a significant landmark for David Adjaye. His rapid rise to prominence has been achieved on the basis of exhibition fit-outs (for example, at the Design Museum and Victoria Miro Gallery, both in London) and lavish domestic interiors, followed by the sensational Elektra House and, more recently, the Dirty House (see pp. 160–62), also both in London. The important public commission for the Idea Store will be a test of Adjaye's ability to work on a large scale and to a tight budget. (Early in 2003 Adjaye was shortlisted for the design of the new British Embassy in Warsaw, Poland – an achievement in itself for a young architect.)

The Idea Store concept clearly develops the philosophy of Will Alsop's Peckham Library in south London, in terms of updating the idea of the public library to fit in with contemporary attitudes and lifestyles. The aim is to demystify it: the way to get people into libraries, it is argued, is to build them in shopping hubs and run them like shops. A library should be not just a repository of knowledge and information, but also an active presence in the community, linked to lifelong learning programmes, that attracts people who would not usually visit such an institution.

The Whitechapel Idea Store forms part of the frontage of one of the East End's main thoroughfares. The five-storey building has shops at street level, with the remainder of the 4500-square-metre floor space consisting of flexible areas in which library and education spaces are mixed. The façade does more than enclose the floors: the curtain wall of coloured and clear glazing and glass-faced aluminium panels is envisaged as a medium for displaying information. (The idea is hardly new: Rogers & Piano wanted to make the piazza frontage of the Pompidou Centre, Paris, into an electronic noticeboard; they were inspired in turn by Oscar Nitschke's unbuilt Maison de la Publicité project of the 1930s.) Inside there is a full-height atrium extending out over the pavement and containing stairs and escalators to draw people up the building. The top floor contains a café with spectacular views over the City and East End. If all this does not demystify the library, nothing ever will.

Above and opposite
Transparent and colourful, Adjaye's Idea Store offers a new image of the public library as an accessible and welcoming place. The project is part of the ongoing regeneration of the eastern fringe of the City.

THE KING'S LIBRARY, BRITISH MUSEUM, WC1

HOK INTERNATIONAL, 2000–03

"The room itself is to be the first exhibit": this was the brief given to HOK by the British Museum when the practice began design work on the restoration and conversion of the King's Library. This noble space, some 91 metres long, was the first part of the British Museum to be constructed (in 1823–27) and it remains the most widely admired of the works of Sir Robert Smirke. Built to house the great library of King George III (containing more than 60,000 volumes) and retaining the splendid original cases made to house the king's books, the King's Library is a Neo-classical masterpiece, comparable with the work of Schinkel in Berlin. Administered in recent years by the British Library, the King's Library was passed back to the museum after the library moved to its new building in St Pancras in 1998, taking George III's books with it. The decision was taken to refurbish the King's Library as a gallery of the Enlightenment (the intellectual revolution that led to the creation of the modern museum) and as an introduction to the museum's vast collections. The opening was scheduled for 2003, marking the 150th anniversary of the British Museum's foundation.

The project (winner of a special conservation award from the RIBA in 2004) is a triumph of tactful restoration, in which modern technology has been seamlessly integrated into a highly sensitive historic ensemble. The fine book presses and floor-mounted display cabinets have been reused (and supplemented by replicas) to display around 3000 objects from the collections, including scientific instruments, sculpture, archaeological and ethnographical items and specimens of natural history. Their adaptation meant inserting air conditioning, fibre-optic lighting and modern security systems. Thousands of spare volumes from the House of Commons library fill some cases, and busts and antique vases are displayed on pedestals: the ambience is that of a great library of the Enlightenment era, where works of art and scientific specimens would commonly be displayed alongside books. The absence of interactive computer terminals and other electronic paraphernalia is particularly welcome: the room and its contents speak for themselves and lead the visitor to explore the collections spread around the museum.

As part of the project, the original Smirke decorative scheme was faithfully restored (with Dr Ian Bristow as consultant) and the marble, granite, scagliola and plasterwork elements as well as the finely crafted timber floor painstakingly cleaned. Although the library may appear untouched by modern interventions, its restoration was a revelation to those who knew it in its previously shabby and crowded state, disfigured by ill-designed British Library displays. For many years the British Museum treated its Grade I-listed building with contempt, but under more inspired leadership it is now making amends. The restoration of the museum's front hall and the Great Court project, which forms a natural complement to the King's Library scheme, equally reflect the fact that Smirke's building is not just a container for objects, but also a magnificent artefact in its own right.

Right and opposite
The King's Library, long recognized as one of the finest interiors in London, has been given a new dimension as a gallery of the Enlightenment. The project included the addition of new cases and the installation of air-conditioning and modern lighting.

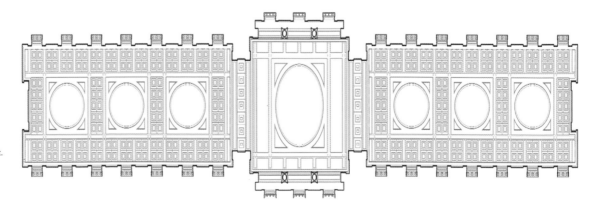

LABAN DANCE CENTRE, CREEKSIDE DEPTFORD, SE8

HERZOG & DE MEURON, 1997–2003

Herzog & de Meuron's Laban Centre is a unique building housing a unique institution. Named after Rudolf Laban (1879–1958), 'the father of modern dance', the centre operated for nearly thirty years from a sprawl of converted buildings in New Cross, a few miles from its new Thameside site at Deptford Creek (formerly a refuse tip). Its removal to Deptford is a component in the strategy to regenerate the area, which was once a centre of shipbuilding – and boasts one of London's finest Baroque churches, Thomas Archer's St Paul's – but is now one of London's poorest districts.

Herzog & de Meuron's 1997 competition victory (Peter Zumthor, Enric Miralles, David Chipperfield and Tony Fretton were among other contenders) came at a time when their Tate Modern project in London was moving from design to construction. Following delays in securing Heritage Lottery funding, the centre was constructed in 2000–02 and formally opened early in 2003.

On a superficial level, the centre can be read as a shed in the local tradition, raised above the mundane by its bold use of external colour (in the form of polycarbonate sheets fixed in front of the glazed façade panels). The revelatory qualities of the building, however, are to be found beyond the façades. The interior is planned around three 'wedges' of circulation space, internal streets intended to encourage creative interaction and a memory of the rambling (but well-loved) collection of buildings that the centre formerly inhabited. Internal courts bring natural light deep into the building and allow views across it. Studios (a total of thirteen, none strictly rectangular) are arranged around the perimeter, while a 300-seat theatre, a facility the centre hitherto lacked, fills the centre of the building. The cafeteria and library are placed along its creekside edge. Two hefty spiral staircases, painted black, provide the principal means of vertical circulation and are seen as places for social encounters. The centre is big-boned, generous and tough, designed to take hard wear from a teaching and learning community that is used to hard work and long hours. This is a creative 'village', intended to reinforce the Laban's established sense of community. The client, led by the centre's director, Marion North, had a strong input in the development of the scheme.

Colour was a vital ingredient from the beginning. Artist Michael Craig-Martin (whom the architects first encountered as a trustee of the Tate) was brought in at an early stage and the strong hues he chose give a sense of orientation and identity to the internal spaces.

Herzog & de Meuron has never been the 'minimalist' practice that some imagine, but the Laban reflects an increasingly expressive element in its architecture that recalls, in some respects, the work of the German architect Hans Scharoun. The full impact of the centre was realized when the remarkable landscape scheme (by Gunther Vogt) was completed in 2004. The Laban Centre can already be regarded as one of the few really significant buildings generated by the cultural building boom of the 1990s.

LONDON REGATTA CENTRE
DOCKSIDE ROAD, E14

IAN RITCHIE ARCHITECTS, 1997–99

The powerful Jubilee line station at Bermondsey aside, Ian Ritchie's built works in London are surprisingly modest in scale – a concert platform at Crystal Palace, for example, and interiors at the Natural History Museum – which is one reason to include his project of the late 1990s here. The Regatta Centre was one of the first new buildings of significant quality to be completed in the long-closed Royal Docks. The site is on Royal Albert Dock, where there is a 2000-metre Olympic-standard rowing course – one good use for a redundant dock.

The Royals are far removed from Henley-on-Thames, and Ritchie's centre is a tough beast made of robust materials and unawed by its setting, yet the detailing is characteristically careful and even delicate. There are, in fact, two buildings here: a clubhouse, with changing rooms, short-stay accommodation and a practice rowing tank, and a boathouse, where up to eighty boats can be stored, plus workshop for repairs and maintenance. The linear form of the complex reflects the nature of the site, squeezed against the water by the elevated track of the Docklands Light Railway. The sharp nose of the clubhouse, highly glazed and open to the dockside, the rear elevation a stark composition in fair-faced concrete, responds to the line of the water. The boathouse is a plain rectangle. Its construction is remarkably straightforward: steel columns, with brackets to support the stored boats, hold up a stainless-steel sheet roof. The walls of the building are gabions – metal cages filled with rough stones. The gabion wall on the north side of the clubhouse encloses a long access spine. This "ambulatory", as Ritchie describes it, is a memorable space: enclosed between rough stonework and smooth concrete, floored in timber and lit from above.

MEDIA CENTRE
LORD'S CRICKET GROUND, NW1

FUTURE SYSTEMS, 1995–99

Older than most of the completed projects included in this book, yet still an astonishingly futuristic sight, the Lord's Media Centre could hardly be described as anything but 'contemporary'. It is the latest of a series of progressive commissions by the Marylebone Cricket Club (MCC), beginning with Michael Hopkins's Mound Stand in the 1980s and including, more recently, Nicholas Grimshaw's effortlessly elegant

Grand Stand, opened in 1998, as well as a number of smaller structures by David Morley Architects (also responsible for the development masterplan for the ground).

The new media centre was planned to open in time for the 1999 Cricket World Cup held at Lord's, providing space for up to one hundred and twenty broadcasters and journalists. An invited competition for its design was held in 1995 and won by

Future Systems, a practice that moved in the 1990s from inspirational ideas to completed buildings. While Hopkins and Grimshaw were recognizably working in an updated version of the engineering tradition of the Victorian period, Future Systems envisaged their building as a lightweight object, prefabricated off-site, like a yacht or aircraft, using a semi-monocoque technique – an aluminium skin forms the

structure of the building, being stiffened with aluminium ribs. The centre sits on two concrete legs, containing stairs and lifts and clad in GRP, between the Compton and Edrich stands (relatively matter-of-fact additions by Hopkins). The external skin is spray-painted a brilliant white. Inside, the commentators' seats are ranged in tiers, like those of the spectators below. The ice-blue colour scheme, apparently somewhat compromised since the opening of the building, was chosen to instil an air of calm (though air conditioning ensures cool conditions). The angled all-glass front of the centre was designed to prevent glare, a potential distraction to players.

This remains Future Systems' largest built project in London. Its smooth, slightly sinister quality makes it unmissable and unforgettable, a "loveable alien", as the *Architects' Journal* described it.

Left
The ranks of seating ensure that the world's press have the clearest possible view of the cricket pitch below.

Opposite
The smooth and striking form of the building's exterior builds on the techniques developed in the construction of aeroplanes and boats.

PECKHAM LIBRARY, PECKHAM SQUARE, SE15
ALSOP ARCHITECTS, 1998–2000

Asked why the Peckham Library and Media Centre is raised twelve metres above Peckham Square, a new public space intended as a focus for community life and regeneration in this underprivileged area of south London, Will Alsop is apt to reply: "why not?" In fact, the logic behind the move becomes apparent to anyone who ascends to the library. There are views not only of the square and surrounding area but also, through the highly transparent, multi-coloured northern elevation, of the public and commercial monuments of the City and West End a few miles away; Peckham's

perceived isolation from central London is revealed as, in fact, an illusion. The overhang of the library shelters part of the square from the weather. Elevated above the streets, the library is both part of the urban fabric and, at the same time, a place appealingly apart, a semi-secret world that has a particular attraction for young people. Public libraries were traditionally seen as places where the masses could be educated and 'improved' – a worthy ideal, but too paternalistic and condescending for the twenty-first century. The Peckham Library is unashamedly colourful, shapely

and sensuous: a container for a new approach to education and information.

The library itself, clad in green patinated copper with a prominent red 'tongue' at roof level, cantilevers out from a five-storey vertical block containing the entrance lobby, offices and staff facilities and a multi-media centre for IT training. Within the reading room, three timber pods set on stilts house a meeting room, children's activity area and a specialist Afro-Caribbean library. The building has presence and glamour, but is far from extravagant; the naturally ventilated interior is equally made for low-cost running.

This is a building for the local community, wearing its serious purpose lightly and reflecting Alsop's conviction that architecture must be interesting, stimulating, unforgettable as well as functional. Peckham Library is all those things and more. It is a building that has a great deal to say about the city, the relationship between learning and enjoyment and the place of art in architecture.

The library's interior provides a new and stimulating environment at the heart of the community in which to read and learn.

Right and below
The north elevation provides a colourful and transparent beacon that looks towards the City and the West End, while the south elevation shelters the new square that has been developed as a focus for this deprived inner-city community.

THE PLACE, DUKE'S ROAD, WC1

ALLIES & MORRISON, 1995–2001

Allies & Morrison's skilful reconstruction of The Place re-equips a well-liked and successful venue for dance without removing its informal and ad hoc character. The 1880s Drill Hall (built for the Artists' Rifles) has been used by the Contemporary Dance Trust since 1969, since when it has expanded its activities into adjacent buildings. The Place is a centre for performance and training, in use from early morning to late in the evening.

Allies & Morrison's involvement with The Place began in 1995, when the practice began work on a masterplan for future development. This led to a £5,000,000 Lottery grant, which was used as the basis for further fundraising. A new entrance for performers and students has been created on Flaxman Terrace, a dramatic triple-height space beyond which dancers can be glimpsed by passers-by. The dance studios have been comprehensively overhauled and equipped with new services.

Right and opposite
The Place, a classic example of the creative use of an old building, has been given a new public face with the addition of a three-storey entrance pavilion, while the existing performance and rehearsal spaces have been refurbished.

THE ROUNDHOUSE, CHALK FARM ROAD, NW1

JOHN McASLAN + PARTNERS, 1998–2004

The Roundhouse is one of the great industrial monuments of London. It was built in 1847 as an engine shed serving the London and Birmingham Railway; redundant within twenty years, it was converted into a warehouse and remained in this use for nearly a century. In 1964 the building passed into the hands of Arnold Wesker's Centre 42 and entered a new incarnation as a venue for experimental theatre, rock music and 'happenings', all of which were in tune with its bare industrial aesthetic. The building was effectively used 'as found': few changes or improvements were made and only the most basic maintenance was carried out. By the 1980s the Roundhouse

was in liquidation, with Camden Council and the GLC stepping in to acquire it. The GLC proposed to use it to establish a centre for black artists, but efforts to secure a permanent purpose for the building came to nothing. More recently Michael Hopkins prepared a scheme to convert it into a home for the RIBA's drawings collection: this would have involved extensive internal change to accommodate large areas of storage space, reading rooms and offices. The use of the building by conceptual artists and performance groups has emphasized the need to protect its spatial qualities.

Philanthropist Torquil Norman bought the Roundhouse in 1998 with the aim of

making it into an arts centre for young people and held a limited competition to select an architect. John McAslan's Lottery-backed project focuses on the retention and restoration of the building's great internal space, to be used as a flexible performance area, with studios in the undercroft. Support facilities are contained within a new, crescent-shaped building, lightly joined to the Roundhouse: the aim is to preserve the great brick drum uncompromised. After decades of uncertainty, this iconic north London landmark appears to have a bright future.

Opposite
Views of working model, showing interior levels (basement, auditorium and mezzanine) and roof.

Right
Interior cutaway view of working model, showing how the insertion of new facilities has been balanced with the desire to retain the internal and external integrity of the historic structure.

ROYAL COURT THEATRE
SLOANE SQUARE, SW3

HAWORTH TOMPKINS ARCHITECTS, 1995–2000

Below
West–east section, showing restaurant beneath Sloane Square, left, and the theatre, right.

A slender new building containing offices and dressing-rooms has been clamped on to the side of the existing building.

Opposite
A characteristic of the refurbishment has been the retention of many of the interior finishes and surfaces, as found, giving the building a rich and varied palette and texture.

The Royal Court Theatre has been famous since the 1950s as a venue for innovative, mould-breaking productions. (It was here that John Osborne's *Look Back in Anger* premiered.) The theatre itself, though listed Grade II, is not of outstanding architectural interest: its fussy 1880s façade makes little impression on Sloane Square and certainly does not challenge the sleekly elegant curve of Peter Jones on the end of the King's Road.

Haworth Tompkins's reconstruction of the theatre confronted a number of difficult issues, quite apart from the confined character of the site. The distressed, not to say scruffy, ambience of the interior was widely seen as part of its charm, and nobody wanted it sanitized. But facilities for English Stage Company staff, performers and audiences were very poor. The scheme added a new six-storey block of dressing-rooms and offices alongside the main building, with more accommodation in a deep basement. The upstairs studio theatre

was totally rebuilt. A considerable slice of the budget went into the construction of a new bar and restaurant under the square (replacing an existing public convenience) with an entrance from the central paved area as well as from the theatre. The local authority's subsequent refusal to allow access from the square was, to say the least, perverse.

The main façade remains largely unchanged, except for cleaning and new lighting. Inside the theatre, the approach was one of stripping back dilapidated and poor-quality finishes, leaving old brickwork and new concrete exposed, so that the interior is a place of rich and memorable texture. A new main staircase is constructed of thin, stepped concrete spans, meticulously detailed. The effect is Scarpa-esque, a contrast to the sleek look of many new/old schemes. Audiences and actors appear to like the rebuilt Court – the spirit of the place lives on.

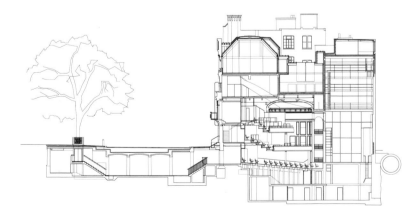

ROYAL FESTIVAL HALL REFURBISHMENT
BELVEDERE ROAD, SE1
ALLIES & MORRISON, 1992–

The appointment of Allies & Morrison to implement a progressive programme of repair and reinstatement at the Royal Festival Hall, the only surviving building from the 1951 Festival of Britain, is one of the key achievements to date of the South Bank Board, which took charge of the entire South Bank Centre after the demise of the Greater London Council (GLC). (The apparent abandonment of Rick Mather's masterplan for the South Bank site has left the Royal Festival Hall stranded in an area that is conspicuously in limbo and beginning to show the detrimental effects of many years of indecision.)

"The prime monument of the Welfare State era", as historian Elain Harwood has described the Grade I listed hall, is a perennially popular, beautifully made and highly subtle building that marries the optimism and drive of the post-war years, when the Modern Movement moved centre-stage in Britain, with the decorative and craft-oriented preoccupations of an older tradition, transmuted via the medium of Scandinavia. The form of the building, with its 'egg in a box' auditorium surrounded by open foyers, was the conception of Leslie Martin, while the interiors were designed by a London County Council (LCC) team led by Peter Moro. Both men were still alive and able to offer advice and encouragement when Allies & Morrison began working on the Royal Festival Hall in the early 1990s. There was general dissatisfaction with the changes implemented by the GLC in 1963–65, which extended the river front of the building, imposing bland new elevations, and wrapped it in a network of walkways and service roads in line with then-current ideas of pedestrian/vehicle segregation. The 'open foyers' policy of the 1980s GLC opened the building to all, from early morning to late evening – today, the majority of the Royal Festival Hall's users never attend a concert there. Peter Moro welcomed this revolution, while deploring the uncontrolled invasion of the public spaces by the shops and cafés that followed the influx of people.

Allies & Morrison (who produced an exceptionally well-considered submission for the 1994 South Bank masterplanning competition) seem to have a natural sympathy with the Royal Festival Hall; their own roots are in the Cambridge school which Leslie Martin made into such a potent architectural force. Their proposals have been developed in conservation plans published in 1996 and 2000. Early phases of work reinstated the character of the original (west) entrance foyer and the progression from entrance to principal level and created an elegant new restaurant overlooking the river. A stretch of 1960s walkway masking the hall from Belvedere Road was removed. There were plans to finally create the grand south entrance that Martin had wanted, but these have since been dropped in favour of a new café opening on to a festival square. It is accepted that the changes of the 1960s cannot be entirely undone, but the reopening of terraces and balconies at the upper levels of the building will recreate something of the openness of the original. A prime objective is the clearance of catering and retail outlets that clutter the public spaces.

Since 1999 Allies & Morrison have worked closely with South Bank masterplanner Rick Mather, since the Royal Festival Hall cannot be detached from its context. The masterplan provides for the suppression of the 1960s service roads around the hall and the insertion, along the edge of the Hungerford railway viaduct, of a new administrative and retail block, designed by Allies & Morrison, which will provide space to decant offices and shops from the Royal Festival Hall. The most daunting element in the £50,000,000 refurbishment scheme is undoubtedly the overhaul of the auditorium, which has acoustics that are now regarded as defective. Plans have been announced to close the hall for a considerable period.

Below

Allies & Morrison's ongoing refurbishment project aims to restore the interior of the Royal Festival Hall in line with the intentions of its original architects and to reverse some of the detrimental changes made since 1951.

Right

The opening of the People's Palace restaurant, along the river front of the building, made good use of one of the spaces created as a result of the 1960s extension, but its style was a deliberate throwback to the lighter aesthetic of 1951.

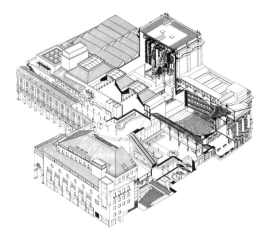

Opposite
The Floral Hall, previously a pathetic remnant, has been partially rebuilt and given a new role as part of the development.

Right
As this cutaway shows, the project involved not only the substantial rebuilding of the opera house, but also the reconstruction of the entire block.

Below
A new internal route, containing the box office, links Covent Garden piazza with Bow Street.

ROYAL OPERA HOUSE COVENT GARDEN, WC2

JEREMY DIXON.EDWARD JONES/ BUILDING DESIGN PARTNERSHIP, 1984–2000

The Royal Opera House is reckoned one of the great opera houses of the world, yet it became the home of a national opera company (and dance company) only after the Second World War. The present theatre is the third to occupy the site, close to the Covent Garden piazza, a pioneering exercise in urban design by Inigo Jones and now the heartland of tourist London. Built in 1857–58 to designs by E.M. Barry, the

Royal Opera House is a much-loved musical shrine. After more than a century of use, however, its facilities proved increasingly inadequate for modern needs. Following twenty years of discussion, the first phase of an extension programme was completed in 1982 by GMW architects, by which time a more ambitious development scheme was being planned. Jeremy Dixon and William Jack (of Building Design

Partnership) won the competition held in 1984, narrowly beating Edward Cullinan and Richard Rogers. After 1989 the project was developed by the partnership of Dixon and Edward Jones, in conjunction with Building Design Partnership (with Charles Broughton as design director). The scheme went through several major transformations before work started on site in 1996 – in its first incarnation, half of the space on the 2.5-acre site was allotted for commercial development, a Thatcherite strategy for funding the development without recourse to public funds that was hotly opposed by community activists. The built scheme, which is devoted, apart from some retail space, to ROH use (the backstage areas are vast), was made possible by a large and controversial Lottery grant, plus substantial private donations.

Jeremy Dixon regards the ROH project as being as much about urban planning as theatre design. It became, he says, "a complex procedure of collaging ... a compressed version of the natural development of a city". One element that remained constant in the various reworkings of the scheme was the run of new façades replacing the long-lost frontages of Inigo Jones's piazza. Where other architects proposed replicas of the vanished original, Dixon produced a reinterpretation in a stripped classical manner. In the angle of the piazza, a new entrance leads into the theatre, restoring an arrangement that prevailed in pre-Barry days.

On Russell Street and Bow Street, the architectural style hangs somewhere

between rationalism and straightforward modern – the disjunction on Russell Street between this manner and that of the piazza frontages is deliberate. On Bow Street, the Barry portico (with a clumsy 1930s conservatory unfortunately left blocking the colonnade) and the restored frontage of the 1860 Floral Hall – which had been half demolished after a 1956 fire – dominate. The idea of using the Vilar Floral Hall (as it became) as a great public foyer for all the house's patrons – breaking down the divisions between the various parts of the auditorium was a key theme of the scheme – was an inspired notion. Yet the fact that it is raised up to allow for a major service entrance on to Bow Street makes it seem inaccessible, and the route into the hall is far from direct. The supposed 'opening up' of the ROH to the general public has been, in the event, rather half-hearted. The most successful element in the reconstruction is the device of an escalator link, whisking patrons direct to a striking top-level bar – but again the route from the street is, perhaps deliberately, indirect. The auditorium, of course, remains unchanged, apart from a repaint and reseating operation, and the mystique and the exclusiveness of the ROH have not been erased by the rebuilding. For London, however, this exercise in Postmodern urban design has real benefits: the piazza façades have an inevitability that made them an immediate and accepted part of the historic Covent Garden scene.

SADLERS WELLS, ROSEBERY AVENUE, EC1

ARTS TEAM @ RHWL/NICHOLAS HARE ARCHITECTS, 1995–98

The arrival of the National Lottery, launched by John Major's otherwise sterile administration, transformed the arts scene in Britain. Popular science centres (Magna, the Earth Centre, Dynamic Earth and so on) blossomed around the country, and in London a massive grant was awarded, amidst considerable controversy, to rebuild the Royal Opera House. The Lottery seemed to be a bottomless coffer.

Under New Labour, the Lottery has been substantially rethought and funds redirected towards projects that might traditionally have been funded from taxation – no more ROH-style spending sprees. Completed as long ago as 1998, the reconstruction of Sadlers Wells demonstrated the potential for fast-track, good-value arts projects, with operational issues more important than those of high style. In this context, it provides a benchmark for the future.

The new Sadlers Wells, opened late in 1998, is the fifth theatre on the site – the first opened in 1683. Its 1931 predecessor, though much-loved, was externally forgettable, internally cramped, and, though listed (for its associations), regarded as expendable. Its context was extremely mixed: across Rosebery Avenue is Berthold Lubetkin's heroic Spa Green Estate. The aim behind the reconstruction was to re-equip the theatre operationally and technically, with vastly improved facilities for audiences and performers; to maintain the special character of the 'Wells' as a local institution, but equally to give it a new image and widen the audience base.

Nicholas Hare's street frontage, with brick planes framing a glazed entrance elevation, does the job efficiently: after dark, the foyer opens up invitingly to the street. The 26-metre-high flytower is not suppressed but frankly expressed as a marker on Rosebery Avenue. At the rear of the building, on Arlington Way, projecting windows break the façade, providing passers-by with glimpses into the interior. Hare is an adept urban compositionalist, and here he is on good form.

Nicholas Thompson of the Arts Team, responsible for the interior of the building, retained the existing placing of the auditorium, keeping part of the structure for purely practical reasons. But the new auditorium is a highly original, slightly frightening place – none of the reassurance, for instance, of Hopkins's Glyndebourne – steeply raked, devoid of traditional frills, starkly clad in perforated metal, its challenging austerity slightly relieved by colourful seat coverings. (But Sadlers Wells, unlike Glyndebourne, is a mould-breaking place.) The foyer is seen as a single space, with lightweight galleries floating in the volume – in practice, this is perhaps a slightly disorientating area, with too many levels and no clear focus of activity. Yet the overall effect of the development is to refresh and reinvigorate an old friend, and the anticipated broadening of horizons has been successful.

SOHO THEATRE, DEAN STREET, W1
PAXTON LOCHER ARCHITECTS, 1996–2000

Lottery funding underpinned a number of high-profile, high-cost arts projects launched in Britain during the late 1990s; the Royal Opera House provides the most striking example in London. The Soho Theatre's Lottery funding was far more modest and the company's translation to a new home was accomplished via a shrewd mix of public funding and straightforward property speculation that allows it to channel such future subsidies as it can raise directly into productions. Its overheads are covered by the revenue from the building.

The company's search for a new base began in 1995, when it was obliged to quit the Cockpit Theatre. It settled on a former synagogue in the heart of Soho, a decent seven-storey block with a sizeable worship space at its core. Paxton Locher, with no previous experience of theatre design, was selected from a shortlist of six practices. The strategy was to place the new, 200-seat auditorium at first- and second-floor level, suspended in space, as it were. The ground floor and basement house the box office, bar and restaurant. The third floor contains rehearsal and administrative space, with apartments on the top three floors (which step back on the rear elevation). The return from the residential development underwrote the project. The result of this approach has been to produce a mixed-use building, a microcosm of the city and a striking contrast to the arts ghettos of the Barbican and South Bank. The ethos of the building suits the company, with its emphasis on new and experimental work and its desire to break out of the traditional theatrical mould.

The changes to the existing building were subtle and respectful: a lightweight canopy to the street, a delicate steel framework denoting the theatre space (with the control room expressed as a box on the street elevation) and a set-back penthouse at roof level. The auditorium is a highly flexible black box, with steeply raked bench seating; the emphasis is on intimacy and communication between audience and actors. Paxton Locher, still best known, perhaps, for their exquisite house and studio in Clerkenwell, proved that specialist experience is not always the route to an inspired job.

THE WOMEN'S LIBRARY, OLD CASTLE STREET WHITECHAPEL, E1

WRIGHT & WRIGHT ARCHITECTS, 1997–2002

Below and opposite
Behind a retained façade inscribed "Wash Houses" – a memory of the old East End of London – the Women's Library is an exquisitely crafted structure in a classic modern tradition. Inside, the emphasis is on careful detail, the controlled use of natural light, and calm and even sober spaces for reading and study.

The Women's Library is not a new institution: the feminist pioneer Millicent Fawcett founded it as long ago as 1926 and it has since evolved as an archive of international importance. The library has belonged to London Guildhall University for a quarter of a century and has finally found a worthy home at the university's Whitechapel campus.

The site is appropriate. The public baths and wash-house that stood there was a place of women's work for more than a century as well as a focus of community life. The 1840s façade, with its inscription "Wash Houses", has been retained as part of the development. Behind it, the new building rises to a total height of six storeys. Apart from a reading room and extensive stacks, the building contains exhibition and seminar spaces, meeting-rooms and a café. The entrance area is a dramatic double-height space, with exhibition areas surrounding a hexagonal lecture theatre, opening on to a garden court on the north side of the building. The exhibition space can accommodate large exhibits – suffragette banners, for example – or act as a break-out area from the lecture room. There is a café at first-floor level behind the arched windows in the retained façade.

This is a carefully crafted building in the Cambridge-rooted modern tradition, which generated, *inter alia*, Colin St John Wilson and Allies & Morrison. Soft red brick, stone, oak and smooth plaster are used internally to create a rich and calm ambience – "an exquisitely crafted casket", as critic Catherine Slessor called it – yet the interior does not lack spatial drama. The solidity of the architecture reflects a serious commitment to energy-saving: heavy insulation and passive cooling devices remove the need for mechanical ventilation, even in archive storage areas. The art programme for the building is ambitious. This is a beautifully wrought, thoughtful and sober building that eschews fashion to make its point: one feels that the leaders of the suffragette movement would have loved it. It is a fine addition to the fabric of the East End.

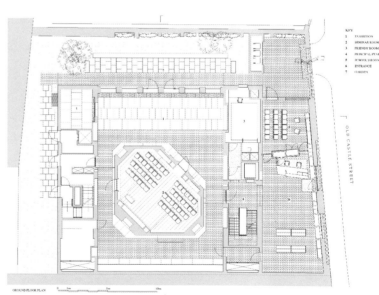

EDUCATION AND HEALTH

ACAD CENTRE, CENTRAL MIDDLESEX HOSPITAL
AVANTI ARCHITECTS

BRIXTON INTERMEDIATE CARE CENTRE
PENOYRE & PRASAD

BUSINESS ACADEMY, BEXLEY
FOSTER AND PARTNERS

CHARTER SCHOOL
PENOYRE & PRASAD

GIRL GUIDES HEADQUARTERS, SOUTH WIMBLEDON
HUGH BROUGHTON ARCHITECTS

HAMMERSMITH HEALTH CENTRE
GUY GREENFIELD ARCHITECTS

HAMPDEN GURNEY PRIMARY SCHOOL
BUILDING DESIGN PARTNERSHIP

JIGSAW DAY NURSERY, WANDSWORTH
WALTERS & COHEN

JUBILEE PRIMARY SCHOOL
ALLFORD HALL MONAGHAN MORRIS

MEDICAL AND DENTAL SCHOOL, QUEEN MARY COLLEGE
ALSOP ARCHITECTS

MOSSBOURNE COMMUNITY ACADEMY
RICHARD ROGERS PARTNERSHIP

**PRIMARY SCHOOL AND HEALTH CENTRE
GREENWICH MILLENNIUM VILLAGE**
EDWARD CULLINAN ARCHITECTS

ROYAL ACADEMY OF MUSIC
JOHN McASLAN + PARTNERS

TANAKA BUSINESS SCHOOL, IMPERIAL COLLEGE
FOSTER AND PARTNERS

TRINITY COLLEGE OF MUSIC
JOHN McASLAN + PARTNERS

UNIVERSITY OF EAST LONDON, DOCKLANDS CAMPUS
EDWARD CULLINAN ARCHITECTS

ACAD CENTRE
CENTRAL MIDDLESEX HOSPITAL
PARK ROYAL, NW10

AVANTI ARCHITECTS, 1995–2000

The ACAD (ambulatory care and diagnostic) centre at Central Middlesex Hospital – once the Willesden Workhouse – is far removed, physically and in spirit, from the global concerns that are driving much of London's architectural scene. The 450-bed hospital serves a slice of north-west London that contains sizeable pockets of deprivation. Its setting, in a largely industrial landscape, is drab. Its buildings are utilitarian, at best, and ill-adapted to the needs of modern medicine. In short, Central Middlesex Hospital, though a well-respected institution, epitomizes the troubled image of Britain's National Health Service.

One new building that costs £12,500,000 cannot compensate for decades of underinvestment, yet Avanti's ACAD centre underlines the potent effect that a single inspirational structure can have on its surroundings and points the way towards continuing renewal of the site. The centre is designed for the diagnosis and

treatment of ambulatory patients (those who do not require a hospital bed – there are no facilities in the building for overnight stays).

The triangular plan of the centre focuses on a central, nine-metre-high 'street', a generous, naturally lit space extending northwards from the spacious reception area (with its stylish coffee bar). West of the central spine is a two-storey treatment wing, with X-ray and other imaging facilities and operating theatres for minor surgery. To the east, consulting and treatment rooms are arranged around open, landscaped courts. The palette of materials for the building is necessarily economical – render, reconstituted stone and timber – but is used with a sure sense of style. Warm colours, judiciously applied, and crisp detailing help to banish memories of dreary NHS interiors. The response of patients and staff to this building has been enthusiastic – it is a tonic in its own right.

Right and opposite
The ACAD centre is a shot in the arm for a tired and dilapidated hospital campus, the stylish and colourful new building focusing on a daylit internal street.

BRIXTON INTERMEDIATE CARE CENTRE PULROSS ROAD, SW9

PENOYRE & PRASAD, 1999–2001

Despite the indisputable problems facing the National Health Service, the last decade has seen serious efforts to improve medical care in the community, with new medical centres established around London to provide a far wider range of services than that offered by the typical local general practitioner's surgery and an alternative to a conventional hospital for relatively straightforward treatments. The outcome has been commissions to a number of excellent architectural practices (Avanti, John Duane, Wharmby Kozdon and Pentarch, for example), but Penoyre & Prasad's centre at Rushton Street, Shoreditch (1997), was one of the best.

The same practice has since completed the £2,300,000 care centre in Brixton, on part of the site of the old South Western Hospital. Penoyre & Prasad's vision is of an architecture that is not only functionally efficient, with up-to-date care facilities, but also welcoming and even therapeutic in character. From the street, the building is

prefaced by a terraced garden, with a glazed entrance façade connecting it to the surrounding neighbourhood. Inside, a café occupies part of the public space, with clinics and treatment rooms opening off it. Short-stay in-patient wards are on the first floor, overlooking a private garden to the rear as well as the public areas to the front. The aim is to offer patients a choice: involvement or privacy. The dining-room 'lantern' has a view down Pulross Road.

The architecture is pragmatic but elegant, with a mix of brickwork, render and timber on a concrete frame. The use of colour and natural timber is part of an agenda to provide a light and inspirational environment for patients and for those who work here. This is a building in the tradition of Berthold Lubetkin and Edward Cullinan (Penoyre & Prasad once worked for the latter) and is a positive contribution to the community in many respects.

Left and opposite
The transparent appearance of the centre opens up the building to the local community, and as such is the antithesis of the perceived image of National Health Service architecture.

BUSINESS ACADEMY, BEXLEY

FOSTER AND PARTNERS, 2001–03

Described as "the first purpose built, part-privately funded independent state school in Europe", the Business Academy at Thamesmead in the London Borough of Bexley is the product of the Labour government's drive to tackle under-achievement in the state education system and to create centres of real excellence in areas where that system is seen to be deficient. In this instance, developer and property magnate Sir David Garrard assumed the role of project sponsor and worked closely with Foster and Partners on the development of the designs for the new building. Around fifty academies are planned around Britain, half of them in London; Foster and Partners has been commissioned to design a further four. The emphasis throughout is on equipping young people to succeed in business and the professions.

For Norman Foster, the project provided the opportunity to develop ideas about school design that he had nurtured over some years. Foster envisaged a school "open-planned, filled with light, democratic and flexible – with no corridors, no institutional barriers and with a philosophy of integration". Opened in two phases in 2002–03 and catering for 1300 pupils aged eleven to eighteen, the Bexley Academy clearly reflects these ideals.

The predominant theme of the three-storey, 11,800-square-metre building is its open planning, with teaching and technical spaces arranged around three courtyard spaces that are places for socializing and interaction: recent thinking about the workplace was clearly an influence here. The business courtyard, which is the academy's principal hub, incorporates a 'trading pit', complete with large plasma screens, where students can get a taste of City-style trading, as well as a café, a theatre and a television studio. The teaching and technical spaces around the courtyards are open-plan, highly flexible and enclosed by moveable partitions. Even spaces that have to be enclosed for safety reasons, such as science laboratories, have fully glazed partitions, ensuring that the theme of transparency and openness is not compromised.

Architecturally, the academy has been described as "a ruthlessly simple box". Its setting is far from glamorous and the area has had serious vandalism problems. By night, closing shutters turn the building into a relatively impregnable box; during working hours it is a beacon of progress for the local community, which makes extensive use of the facilities outside school hours. The double-skin façades, with shading louvres to baffle solar gain, are part of a low-energy services agenda to cut running costs and increase the overall sustainability rating of the building.

Given the aims of the academy, it is entirely appropriate that the building draws on Foster and Partners' wide experience of office design: why should a school be a place divorced from the world of work? Disciplined, quietly elegant and purposeful, this is a building with a mission.

CHARTER SCHOOL, RED POST HILL, SE21

PENOYRE & PRASAD, 1999–2002

"Education, education, education": one of the key themes of the Blair government, which has expressed a determination to address the problem of under-achieving pupils and under-achieving schools. Clearly, wholesale demolition of failing schools is not a practical option. Penoyre & Prasad's makeover of the old premises of Dulwich High School for Boys (formerly William Penn School) to house the new Charter School suggests an alternative approach.

The Charter School is a new comprehensive serving local children (who were previously obliged to attend schools across the borough) from a diverse social background, and it had hardly opened (in September 2000) before its first 180 places were oversubscribed by 500%. The bold and colourful new environment of the school has undoubtedly been part of the success story. One element in the formula was the creation of a real social heart with a sense of identity and community.

Penoyre & Prasad's raw material was a decent, if tired, campus of five detached buildings designed by LCC architects in the mid-1950s. The architecture had elegance, but it was austere and stranded in a bleak landscape. In terms of environmental performance, it did not meet modern standards. Its buildings were designed around an open courtyard – Penoyre & Prasad's key move was to roof over this space to create a covered atrium, an all-weather social forum, its roof supported on steel 'trees' painted green. The result is a solid, almost industrial aesthetic. The school is approached along a new landscaped 'boulevard' and entered at a single point, marked by a curving red wall, directly into the new atrium. The pedestrian route continues across the site connecting to new glazed routes between the buildings across landscaped courtyards. New lifts, strongly expressed within coloured shafts, provide access to levels for all pupils. Colour has been used boldly throughout. It is planned to reclad all the buildings in later phases of the project, with the reduction of energy and maintenance costs a clear objective. (The use of photovoltaic collectors is envisaged.) Although the architects tackled only two blocks, refurbishment of other blocks and the construction of further glazed routes is also planned.

This is a fine example of architectural transformation, achieved within public spending guidelines and with respect for the existing architectural context. The incisiveness of Penoyre & Prasad's approach, however, reflects the determination of all involved to create an outstanding new school. It is encouraging to see a practice of this calibre developing its portfolio of public commissions.

Left and opposite
At Charter School, Penoyre & Prasad have revitalized a worn-out campus of 1950s buildings, providing covered links and a new central atrium, its roof supported on rugged steel 'trees'.

GIRL GUIDES HEADQUARTERS
SOUTH WIMBLEDON, SW19
HUGH BROUGHTON ARCHITECTS, 1999–2000

The total cost of Hugh Broughton's elegant but robust headquarters for the South Wimbledon District Girl Guides (membership: two hundred and rising) was £189,916. The building is at the other end of the scale from many of the major public projects of the recent past, supported, as was this project, by Lottery grants. Yet its significance is all the greater: an inconspicuous building in an obscure suburb could easily have been a purely functional amenity. Broughton's building is a delight.

The guides previously used a former army hut, which steadily became unusable, on a site locked in by adjacent developments. The brief to the architects was to design a new hall that could be let to other local groups, with kitchen, lavatories, committee room and store, all accessible to the disabled. Low maintenance and running costs were vital.

The completed building is straightforward: a steel-framed rectangle, largely glazed on the south front (which faces an open green space) on a brick base, with untreated cedar also used as a facing material. The monopitch roof, supported on slender trusses, is of corrugated steel.

Designing for children is a challenge: condescension comes easily. There is nothing twee or juvenile about this building, but it is designed with its users in mind. A long timber bench along the garden front, for example, comes in useful for out-of-door activities. Cedar *brise-soleils* guard against excessive solar gain.

The Lottery charities board gave £158,560 for this project: the remainder was raised by the guides.

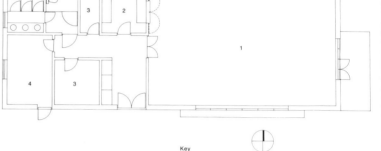

Key

1   Hall
2   Kitchen
3   Store
4   Committee Room

South Wimbledon District Guides Headquarters
Ground Floor Plan

Hugh Broughton Architects

Above and opposite
The Girl Guides centre in South Wimbledon is an example of a stylish but highly practical building designed and built to a tight budget and making good use of simple materials.

Opposite, top
From inside the building there are only oblique
views of the busy road, while a highly glazed
façade overlooks an enclosed inner courtyard.

Opposite, bottom
The interior is characterized by a skilful use of
natural and artificial light and cool colouring.

Below
Situated at the Hammersmith roundabout, and
facing the flyover, the building presents a
deliberately defensive if elegant façade that defers
to the imagery of sailing and the nearby river.

HAMMERSMITH HEALTH CENTRE, W6
GUY GREENFIELD ARCHITECTS, 1996–2000

The centre of Hammersmith has never recovered from two disasters: the construction of the monstrous, polluting flyover and associated road links in the 1960s (would it have happened in Belgravia?) and the abandonment of Norman Foster's visionary transport interchange project (1977–80). It is now dominated by a dreary Postmodernist shopping and office centre, some packing case hotels and, of course, the flyover. The large, dull Victorian church of St Paul makes little impact in this context, though its immediate setting has been much improved in recent years by the creation of a small but pleasant park, and some efforts have been made, very belatedly, to tame the traffic and give pedestrians some rights. For all that, it is a dire spot.

Guy Greenfield's health centre, white and curvy, and with real value for the local community, is therefore a tonic for Hammersmith. It stands close to the church, on a busy traffic roundabout, hence the lack of windows on the street front. The architects were appointed in 1996 by the local health authority, and the building houses a large and busy medical group practice.

The eye-catching form of the centre is not merely arbitrary, but is designed to respond to the landscape of the new park and to baffle noise from the road. Inside, a corridor forms an additional barrier between the exterior and the medical consulting rooms, giving passers-by an oblique glimpse into the building across planted areas. A generous entrance area, further filtering the grime of the streets, leads to the reception lobby. A strong emphasis has been laid on clarity and legibility. Views out to the internal courtyard, with its Japanese-style garden, have a calming effect. The use of colour and natural materials – slate floors, for example, in public areas – is equally cheering. The project is rooted in a belief that surroundings matter to patients – a lesson that could be lost as the NHS pursues the course of Private Funding Initiative financing in the name of value for money.

HAMPDEN GURNEY PRIMARY SCHOOL, MARYLEBONE, W1

BUILDING DESIGN PARTNERSHIP, 1995–2002

Sir Arthur Conan Doyle's fictional detective Sherlock Holmes famously referred to the board schools of Victorian London as "beacons of the future". Towering above the humble terraced streets and often with playgrounds on the roof, these citadels of learning, according to Holmes, presaged a more civilized society.

Building Design Partnership's (BDP) Hampden Gurney Primary School marks, in one sense, a return to tradition. Post-war schools, even in inner London, have tended to be low-rise, but Hampden Gurney, like the old board schools, is a multi-level school and has playing areas set high above the streets. Yet in other respects – in its transparency, lightness and flexibility –

it is a radical design, far removed from the rigidly compartmented academies of the nineteenth century.

The site was formerly occupied by a typical low-rise school of the 1950s, built inexpensively on land cleared by wartime bombing – a gash in the densely built-up area. Plans for a new school came to fruition in 1995, when BDP was appointed to design it after competitive interviews. The school itself is now framed by two housing blocks, also designed by BDP, that help to cement it into its context and were vital to the funding package.

The diagram of the building is clear and practical. The ground floor contains a nursery area, plus offices and staff room.

From here, pupils progress literally 'up the school': the top floor has a technology garden for those in year six. An assembly hall and a chapel (since this is a Church of England school) are located at basement level, together with a playground for ball games. Other play areas, which can be used for open-air teaching in fine weather, are provided on the street front at each level. They are connected to the classrooms by bridges across the void that extends through the centre of the building and is a source of natural ventilation. A tensile fabric canopy extends above the atrium and provides some shelter for the rooftop play area. The openness of the steel-framed building reflects some skilful structural

engineering (also by BDP), with a rooftop bow arch picking up the floor loadings.

Directly commissioned by the end-user, this school shows that private finance initiatives (PFIs) are not the only, or the best, way to procure new education buildings. It is a revelation – the best new school in the capital for some years. This makes the delays imposed by the local authority, Westminster City Council (planning permission took three years to secure), all the more lamentable.

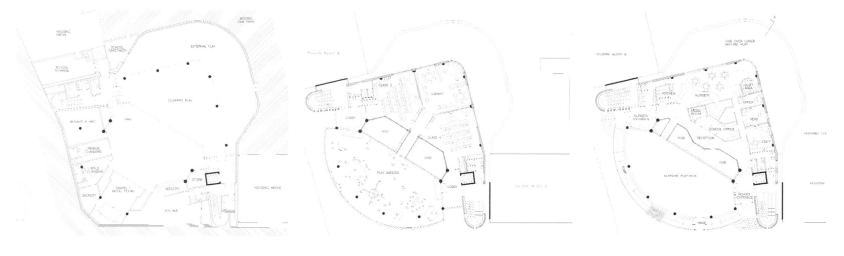

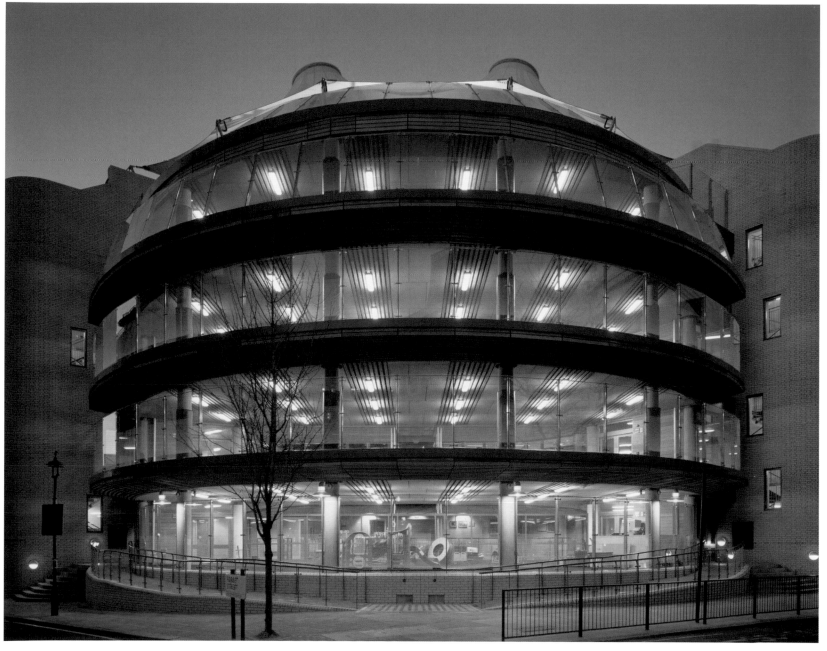

JIGSAW DAY NURSERY, WANDSWORTH, SW18

WALTERS & COHEN, 2000–2001

Founded in 1994 by Cindy Walters and Michal Cohen, Walters & Cohen has acquired a reputation for fastidious detailing, an inspired use of materials and the ability to achieve wonders on modest budgets. Like many other young practices, it has lived to some extent on commissions for private houses and office fit-outs. Its abilities have come to the fore, however, in a series of nursery schools designed for Jigsaw Day Nurseries plc, a company that has successfully capitalized on the demand, largely from young professionals, for high-quality childcare. The first project for Jigsaw, in Bristol, was completed in 1997, with a second scheme, at Stockley

Park, near Heathrow, following a year later; both schemes successfully overcame the potential hurdle of design-and-build contracts.

The Wandsworth nursery is very different, in that it is not a new building but a fit-out of space in a relatively run-of-the-mill luxury housing development close to Wandsworth Bridge. It fits easily into a run of shops and restaurants. The nursery facilities are housed in a series of pods – flexible spaces that can be opened up or enclosed as the activities in hand demand. The double-height space in which they sit provided scope for a mezzanine retreat for staff. A garden, designed by the architects,

is a natural extension of the internal space: the opportunity to play in the fresh air is seen as an important asset. One of the most striking features of the project is the extensive use of natural materials: the birch-faced ply, for example, used to clad the pods, and the timber furniture. On one level, the nursery provides a natural environment for the privileged youngsters who will be the trend-setters of the future. But it also offers a model for nursery provision more generally: its avoidance of the clichés of 'child-centred' design is very welcome.

Below and opposite
The nursery, housed in an unremarkable commercial development, demonstrates a clever use of scale and natural materials, providing a friendly environment for children.

JUBILEE PRIMARY SCHOOL, TULSE HILL, SW2

ALLFORD HALL MONAGHAN MORRIS, 2000–02

Below
The diagram of the Jubilee Primary School places juniors on the first floor of the building, with infants and nursery classes below.

Opposite
The dignity and directness of the building is in the tradition of the classic schools of the immediate post-war era.

A project won in competition by Allford Hall Monaghan Morris (AHMM), the Jubilee Primary School follows on from the practice's much-discussed school at Great Notley in Essex, completed in 1999 and particularly notable for its sustainable servicing strategy.

The Jubilee Primary School was commissioned by Lambeth Council as one of four large new primary schools in the south London borough. The site was formerly occupied by Brockwell Primary School but was far from large. Apart from the main 420-pupil infant and primary school, it had to accommodate a special-needs unit for deaf children and a crèche for children under three years old. Facilities for the local community also had to be provided.

The success of the project is rooted in its strong diagram, with the hall (widely used by local people outside school hours) forming a dramatic presence on the street; a blue brick wall marks the main entrance to the school. The classrooms are arranged in a single block along the northern edge of the site: juniors are on the first floor, nursery and infant classes below. Playground areas can be accessed directly from both levels. The special-needs unit is located at the quietest corner of the site, with its own entrance. The southern part of the site is devoted to open play areas.

Low running costs were a prime objective: light and ventilation chimneys serve the classrooms. Recycled materials have been used widely, and the classroom block has an insulating sedum roof.

The school's showpiece status was reinforced by the commissioning of Studio Myerscough to develop signage and a brand identity, and of Andrew Stafford to design bespoke furniture. Artist Martin Richman collaborated with the architects on a number of elements in the scheme. The school was an appropriate project for completion during the royal Golden Jubilee year of 2002. Fifty years ago schools – for example, Bousfield School, South Kensington, by Chamberlin, Powell & Bon, and Hallfield School, Bayswater, by Denys Lasdun – were among the finest products of the post-war renewal programme. AHMM's building is worthy to stand comparison with these iconic works.

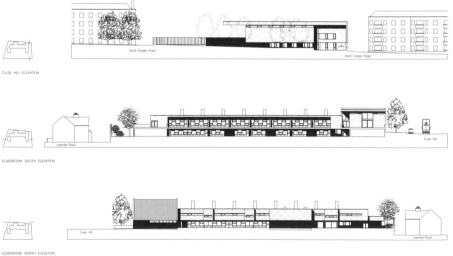

MEDICAL AND DENTAL SCHOOL
QUEEN MARY COLLEGE, UNIVERSITY OF LONDON
WHITECHAPEL, E1

ALSOP ARCHITECTS, 2001–

Below
Will Alsop's new medical school includes an interactive science centre, open to the public and visible within the glazed pavilion of the building.

Opposite
The building is innovative in its provision of interactive space – vital in a modern research facility – and breaks with the idea of medical buildings as anonymous and secretive.

Will Alsop's new medical and dental school for Queen Mary College, University of London, will house the combined schools of St Bartholomew's and the Royal London hospitals on a site adjacent to the latter in Whitechapel, east London. The building, with 9000 square metres of floor space, will contain research laboratories, teaching spaces, lecture theatres, offices and a café, as well as an innovative interactive science centre intended to be used by local schools. This will be the first publicly accessible facility within any British medical school – perhaps a place where the doctors of the future will discover their vocation.

Medical schools, like hospitals, are specialized buildings, usually designed by practices with extensive experience in the field. As a result they are often dire architecturally. For this project Alsop teamed up with AMEC and drew on the latter's expertise in laboratory design to produce a scheme that transforms the image of medical buildings as drab and anonymous. This school is intended as a statement of the dynamic nature of medical research, a place where traditional barriers are removed.

The heart of the building is, in fact, a public space or 'street' overlooked by the café – further reflecting the move to involve the local community in medical research and teaching – and flanked by a great wall of services. All laboratory space is concentrated on one huge floorplate at lower-ground level, extending across the entire site. Specialist research laboratories occupy enclosed cells around the open-plan teaching areas. The glazed pavilion, clad with a double-skin curtain wall, that gives the building its potent presence on the street contains write-up, seminar and office areas on three upper floors. Alsop's characteristic pods and free-form spaces allow views through the building and encourage interaction and socialization by students and staff. The science centre stands within the pavilion, clearly visible from the outside. A 400-seat lecture theatre is sited on the opposite side of the central street. The building is intended as "a backdrop of light and art" to the very serious activities that it houses, but it is a highly practical container, designed for flexibility in the rapidly changing world of research. It should be a place of inspiration: it could be one of the most exciting London buildings of the early twenty-first century, and it is particularly encouraging that it is sited in London's East End.

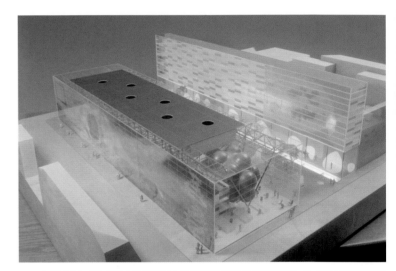

MOSSBOURNE COMMUNITY ACADEMY
DOWNS ROAD, HACKNEY, E5

RICHARD ROGERS PARTNERSHIP, 2002–04

Mossbourne Academy is a new sort of school in several respects. One of a new breed of city academies, designed to provide a shot in the arm for the state sector, it aims to equip pupils for careers in business and industry and, like other academies, is partly financed by a private sponsor. In the case of Mossbourne, backing came from Clive Bourne, a highly successful businessman born in Hackney, who made it a condition of his donation that Rogers be commissioned to design the £23 million new school, and also stipulated that it specialize in communications and information technology. Places at the school are already heavily oversubscribed.

Designed to accommodate some nine hundred students aged from eleven to sixteen, the academy replaces an existing failed school on the same triangular site (which faces the green parkland of Hackney Downs to the north but is enclosed by busy railway lines on two sides). The V-shaped plan opens to the Downs, with two wings of accommodation pressed hard against the rail tracks; the simply rendered rear elevations are virtually windowless and services and support areas buffer the teaching spaces against noise. Classrooms and other teaching areas are accessed from the north via staircases and galleries/cloisters. The aim was to minimize circulation space: nothing here of the central 'street' that is a feature of the academy in Bexley designed by Foster

and Partners. The building is conceived as a series of vertical units, comparable to terraced houses, which provide pupils and staff with a home base; there is, for example, no central staff room.

This is the first timber-framed building (using mostly laminated softwood) designed by Richard Rogers Partnership: the lightweight structure sits on the rubble from the 1960s buildings that formerly stood on the site. The project is intended as an exemplar of sustainable design. Most spaces are entirely naturally ventilated, with rooftop wind towers drawing in fresh air. Solar shading and the use of concrete floors as thermal reservoirs reinforce the low-energy services strategy.

The academy is intended as a resource for the whole community, with the building accessible outside school hours: the sports hall and flexible performance space are heavily used. With school uniforms designed by Paul Smith and a cafeteria menu supervised by the River Café, pupils at Mossbourne might appear to be a privileged élite, yet Hackney is London's most deprived borough and the Mossbourne experiment is a bold attempt to address social inequalities. This is a project that the Rogers team addressed with evident relish, producing a building that wears its earnestness lightly and is already being much enjoyed by those who work and study there.

Opposite, top
The academy occupies a constricted
site hemmed in by railways.

Opposite, bottom and below left
A rare example of a timber-framed structure,
the building stands on the rubble of the
previous 1960s school.

Below right
Internally, the stress is on flexibility
and openness, with a bold use of colour.

PRIMARY SCHOOL AND HEALTH CENTRE GREENWICH MILLENNIUM VILLAGE, SE10

EDWARD CULLINAN ARCHITECTS, 1998–2001

Another project from a long-established practice that still designs with the enthusiasm of youth. The brief for the project was strongly practical – a school for 420 children, aged four to eleven, with provisions for those with special educational needs and facilities for the extended local community in a large attached hall, and a well-equipped district health centre – and highly innovative. The inter-connected buildings address the ambitious agenda for new sustainable urban communities, developed on brownfield sites, set out in the 1999 Urban Task Force report. They equally reflect new ideas of integrating educational, health and other community services in complexes that provide the urban villages of the future with a recognizable public focus.

The site is at the north-west entrance to the Millennium Village, on the pedestrian route to the Dome; the circular hall is seen as a gatepost to the residential development. The buildings are arranged around and entered from a piazza, with the more private classrooms and consulting and treatment rooms facing south into enclosed gardens and play areas. Extensive shading protects these spaces from direct sunlight in summer. The use of an innovative passive cooling system ensures comfortable conditions, while high levels of insulation cut winter heating bills. Materials are conspicuously natural – lots of timber on a steel frame – and used in a straightforward Cullinan way, without recourse to mere folksiness. The walls of English larch enclosing the piazza are reassuring in the, as yet, bleak landscape of the Greenwich peninsula, which was within living memory the site of Europe's largest gasworks.

The protracted controversy over the Dome has obscured the significance of the wider regeneration programme that is transforming the surrounding area. Cullinan's optimistic and cheerful architecture confounds the sceptics and points the way towards the rebirth of London's forgotten backyard.

Opposite, above and right
This development includes a range of community facilities forming a social focus for the new housing on the Greenwich peninsula, and makes use of a broad palette of largely natural materials.

ROYAL ACADEMY OF MUSIC
MARYLEBONE ROAD, NW1

JOHN McASLAN + PARTNERS, 1998–2001

The Royal Academy of Music is England's oldest centre of musical training, founded in 1823 under the patronage of George IV. It moved to the Marylebone Road in 1912, to a new building designed by Sir Ernest George, with teaching rooms, offices and a concert hall, the Duke's Hall. The academy has had several phases of expansion since, including the radical conversion of a war-damaged Nash terrace on York Gate. McAslan's development scheme seeks to weld together the disparate elements of the institution to form an attractive central London campus.

The challenge of the site, a gap between listed buildings close to Regent's Park, was matched by that of the client brief, which called for new teaching and practice rooms, a museum to house the academy's remarkable collection of manuscripts and historic instruments, and a small concert hall capable of being used for recording sessions.

McAslan's solution has been to sink the concert hall, seating 175, into the site, from which it emerges as a long barrel-vaulted form. A new central square for the academy is formed around this intervention.

Right
The project provides for a new concert hall, seen under construction below, slotted in to the gap between the original building of 1912 and the converted terrace on York Gate.

Opposite
The York Gate terrace has been radically refurbished to provide greatly improved rehearsal facilities.

TANAKA BUSINESS SCHOOL, IMPERIAL COLLEGE
SOUTH KENSINGTON, SW7

FOSTER AND PARTNERS, 2002–04

Imperial College – effectively the British equivalent of the Massachusetts Institute of Technology – occupies a crowded site in South Kensington, between the Albert Hall and the Science and Natural History museums. During the 1960s T.E. Collcutt's magnificent Imperial Institute, except for its landmark tower, was demolished to allow for the expansion of the college. Some fine town houses by the late nineteenth-century architect Richard Norman Shaw were also flattened. Unfortunately, most of the new buildings subsequently developed by Imperial College were of mediocre quality. In more recent years the college has raised its sights: John McAslan has refurbished and extended the library, for example.

Foster and Partners' involvement with the college developed from the practice's work early in the 1990s on Albertopolis,

a masterplan for the entire South Kensington museum and education quarter. As part of a subsequent development plan for Imperial College, Foster designed the Sir Alexander Fleming Building (1994–98), a structure of outstanding quality housing medical research and teaching facilities. The next Foster addition was the Flowers Building, containing multi-disciplinary research space and slotted into a tight backland site adjacent to the Science Museum's Wellcome Wing.

The Tanaka Business School, in contrast, is prominently located on Exhibition Road: the project is linked to a radical reconstruction of the college's main entrance. Part of the accommodation is contained within a refurbished 1920s block, while a new stainless-steel drum, housing banks of lecture rooms, makes an arresting addition to the streetscape.

Left top and centre, and opposite
The Tanaka Business Centre gives Imperial College an imposing 'front door'. Inside, a striking steel drum houses banks of lecture theatres.

Left, bottom
The Alexander Fleming building, one of a number of other buildings by Foster and Partners on the college campus.

TRINITY COLLEGE OF MUSIC
GREENWICH, SE10

JOHN McASLAN + PARTNERS, 1999–2001

Trinity College of Music, one of Britain's leading musical academies, was one of the beneficiaries when the Royal Naval College moved out of the former Royal Hospital in Greenwich. The imposing Baroque complex, begun in 1662 and intended initially as a royal palace but completed as a home for retired seamen, was the work of John Webb, Christopher Wren, Nicholas Hawksmoor and John Vanbrugh; the Royal Naval College took over the site in 1873. Listed Grade I and awarded ancient monument status, the buildings, including some of the finest in Britain, are part of a World Heritage Site.

With 600 students formerly housed in a number of buildings in central London, Trinity College was allocated the King Charles Building, the first of the blocks at Greenwich to be begun (by Webb) but only completed well into the eighteenth century. The Royal Hospital includes several magnificent interiors, notably the Painted Hall and a chapel, but most of the blocks contained utilitarian accommodation for aged seafarers. Over the last century most of the original fit-out had been removed, opening the way for the stripping out of later partitions to create rehearsal rooms, offices, a library and social spaces.

Given a relatively modest budget – £7,750,000 for 7500 square metres – the project had to be matter of fact, with few trimmings. Services are generally left frankly exposed and surface-mounted. Ventilation is provided simply by opening windows. The skeleton of the building is able to withstand the heavy wear it will inevitably sustain. The juxtaposition of the old structure with new interventions is one of the most satisfying aspects of reuse projects such as this: at Greenwich it is seen to good effect in the top-floor Jerwood Library, where the great timber roof trusses have been left open to view.

There is a sense in this project of Trinity College simply inhabiting the historic building – conversion has not taken place. This is appropriate for the Greenwich site because it has already been through several changes of function, and the music students may not be there forever. However, McAslan has drawn up plans for a second, more ambitious phase of development in which the central court of the building would be covered with a glazed roof, giving the college a large sheltered social and performance space. This proposal waits on funding and the necessary consents.

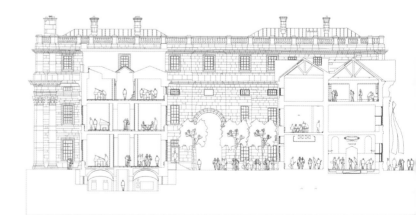

Right
Trinity College is housed in part of the finest complex of Baroque buildings in Britain.

Opposite
The conversion was both economical and respectful to the historic interiors: in the top-floor library, magnificent oak trusses have been opened up to view.

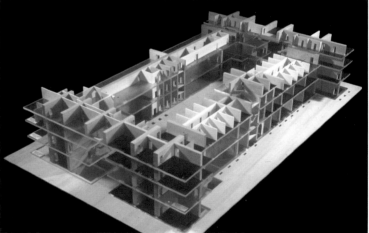

UNIVERSITY OF EAST LONDON
DOCKLANDS CAMPUS, E16

EDWARD CULLINAN ARCHITECTS, 1997–99

Below and opposite
The strong cylindrical forms and bold use of
colour of the residential and teaching blocks, built
to a tight schedule and budget, add visual interest
to the vast and largely empty expanses of the
Royal Docks.

Given the social conviction, humane
pragmatism and youthful verve of its
completed projects in the capital (beginning
with Ted Cullinan's own marvellous low-
budget house, completed in 1964), Edward
Cullinan Architects has built far too little in
London. The new campus for the University
of East London in the Royal Docks is a
visual delight, as it needs to be. The pace
of development in the Royals has been
slow, with the 1990s recession scuppering
some major projects: a lack of adequate
transport infrastructure, only partly
addressed by the Docklands Light Railway,
has been an obvious problem. Premature
clearance of existing buildings, some with
great potential for reuse, has created
daunting expanses of emptiness. The first
two decades of the new century, however,
should see the Royals boom. Cullinan's
campus may soon cease to be an outpost.

The site is alongside the Royal Albert
Dock, close to the Dockland Light Railway's
Cyprus station and facing London City
Airport across the water. Locating an
educational campus here was seen as a
way of stimulating development, including
investment in scientific research facilities,
and twenty-eight start-up units were
included in the scheme. The project was
funded by an alliance of public and private
interests and built to a tight budget on the

basis of a 'develop-and-construct' contract,
with details formulated by the contractor.
The campus was built in eighteen months.

The brief was for a masterplan providing
for a campus to accommodate 7000
students: the first phase was to
accommodate 2400 in eight departments,
with 384 residential places. The
monumental scale of earlier buildings in
the Royals was clearly unachievable:
instead, Cullinan opted for strong form
and vivid colour, plus a decisive landscape
strategy, to create a sense of identity and
place. The academic departments are
arranged as a south-facing 'cliff', with the
residences arranged as free-standing four-
storey drums, coloured green, yellow or
blue, around a public square. The low-
energy ventilation/heating system was
developed (with engineers Whitby & Bird)
in response to an environment where noise
from the City Airport is a major issue.

This scheme demonstrates the potential
of the newest universities to venture where
older institutions would fear to tread. It also
shows the skill of the architects to secure
exemplary results with a procurement
process that often produces banality.
This is good, practical design for a classic
'brownfield' location, with a generous dose
of delight thrown in.

HOUSING

ARSENAL FOOTBALL CLUB REDEVELOPMENT
ALLIES & MORRISON

BEDZED, CROYDON
BILL DUNSTER ARCHITECTS

BRICK LEAF HOUSE, HAMPSTEAD
WOOLF ARCHITECTS

COOKSON SMITH HOUSE, TWICKENHAM
EDWARD CULLINAN ARCHITECTS

DIRTY HOUSE, WHITECHAPEL
ADJAYE ASSOCIATES

ELEKTRA HOUSE, WHITECHAPEL
ADJAYE ASSOCIATES

GARNER STREET HOUSE, BETHNAL GREEN
FAT

HOUSE, 125 GOLDEN LANE
USE ARCHITECTS (JO HAGAN)

HOUSE, 180 HIGHBURY HILL
CHARLES THOMSON/RIVINGTON STREET STUDIO

HOUSE, TITE STREET
TONY FRETTON ARCHITECTS

HOUSING, COIN STREET
HAWORTH TOMPKINS ARCHITECTS

KEELING HOUSE REFURBISHMENT, CLAREDALE STREET
MUNKENBECK & MARSHALL

KNIGHT HOUSE, RICHMOND UPON THAMES
DAVID CHIPPERFIELD ARCHITECTS

LONDON TOWN: 44 HOPTON STREET
KEVIN DASH ARCHITECTS/GAMUCHDJIAN ASSOCIATES

MILLENNIUM VILLAGE HOUSING, GREENWICH
ERSKINE TOVATT/EPR/PROCTOR MATTHEWS ARCHITECTS

PEABODY HOUSING, MURRAY GROVE
CARTWRIGHT PICKARD ARCHITECTS

PRIORY HEIGHTS, PRIORY GREEN ESTATE
AVANTI ARCHITECTS

10–22 SHEPHERDESS WALK
BUSCHOW HENLEY

STRAW HOUSE AND QUILTED OFFICE, STOCK ORCHARD STREET
SARAH WIGGLESWORTH ARCHITECTS/JEREMY TILL

TALL HOUSE, WIMBLEDON
TERRY PAWSON

VXO HOUSE, HAMPSTEAD
ALISON BROOKS ARCHITECTS

ARSENAL FOOTBALL CLUB REDEVELOPMENT
AVENELL ROAD, N5

ALLIES & MORRISON, 2000–06

Arsenal Football Club's (not uncontentious) decision to relocate its ground to Ashburton Grove, some distance from the existing Highbury stadium, with a new £300,000,000 state-of-the-art stadium designed by HOK Sport, posed the question of what could be done with the stands at Highbury, one of which (the Avenell Road east stand) is listed.

Early in 2000 Allies & Morrison was asked to produce proposals for the reuse of the Highbury site, with the emphasis on residential development. The idea of converting a football ground to a new residential quarter is entirely novel, yet the proposed solution seems completely rational and could produce something unique. The east and west stands are to be converted into residential space, with highly transparent, curtain-walled elevations overlooking the former pitch area, which is to be relandscaped as a series of enclosed gardens, with a car park at basement level. The overhanging stand roofs provide a

convenient means of shading these elevations. Inside the stands, existing foyer areas are to be retained as entrances to the blocks. The present north and south stands, which are of no special interest, are to be demolished and replaced by new residential blocks, smaller in scale than the retained stands but sufficiently tall to retain the sense of enclosure that is a prime characteristic of the ground. Double-height living spaces are intended to make maximum use of the attractive setting.

It is proposed to create an improved route into the site from Arsenal station, with a low-rise development of mews-style houses, plus some light industrial space, a token nod, perhaps, to the prescription for mixed-use development. The inclusion of a significant quantity of affordable housing is a welcome and necessary ingredient in what is a highly commercial development, intended to underwrite the club's investment in a new venue for Premier League football.

Right and opposite
As part of the proposal to convert Arsenal's famous ground to residential use, two of the former stands will become apartment buildings, while the pitch will be transformed into a series of enclosed gardens, with car parking beneath.

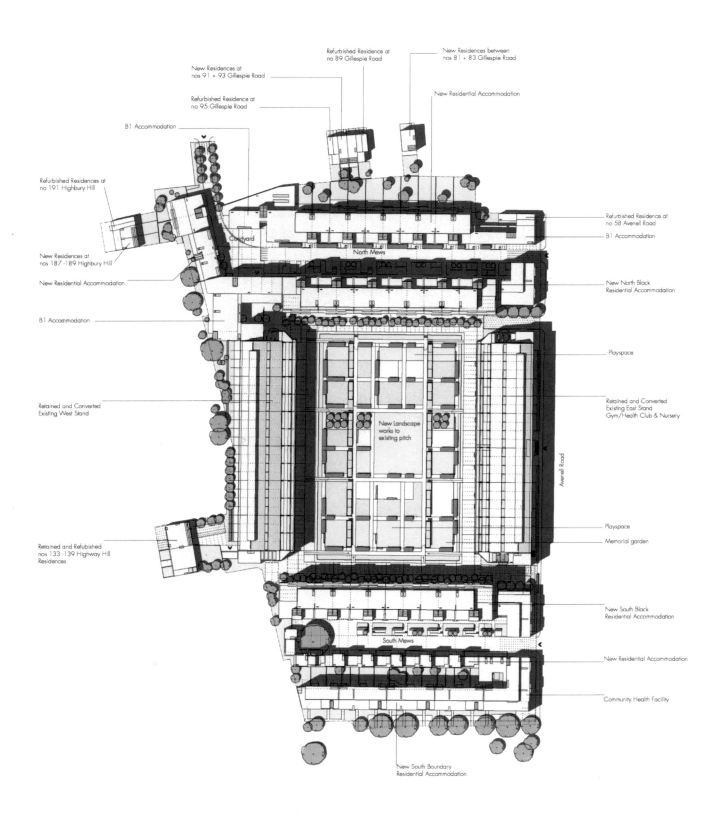

New Residences at
nos 91 + 93 Gillespie Road

Refurbished Residence at
no 89 Gillespie Road

New Residences between
nos 81 + 83 Gillespie Road

Refurbished Residence at
no 95 Gillespie Road

New Residential Accommodation

B1 Accommodation

Refurbished Residences at
no 191 Highbury Hill

Refurbished Residence at
no 58 Avenell Road

B1 Accommodation

Courtyard

North Mews

New North Block
Residential Accommodation

New Residences at
nos 187 -189 Highbury Hill

New Residential Accommodation

B1 Accommodation

Playspace

Retained and Converted
Existing West Stand

Retained and Converted
Existing East Stand
Gym/Health Club & Nursery

New Landscape
works to
existing pitch

Avenell Road

Playspace

Retained and Refubished
nos 133 -139 Highway Hill
Residences

Memorial garden

New South Block
Residential Accommodation

South Mews

New Residential Accommodation

Community Health Facility

New South Boundary
Residential Accommodation

BEDZED, CROYDON
BILL DUNSTER ARCHITECTS, 1999-2002

Located on the southern edge of Greater London, BedZED – Beddington zero energy development – occupies part of the site of a former sewage works. The context is that of low-rise suburbia, though at a density of one hundred units per hectare it provides a persuasive model for new housing on inner-city brownfield sites.

BedZED was effectively a test-bed for radical ideas about sustainability in mass housing, with the ever-pioneering Peabody Trust as developer. It was designed as a socially mixed development for around seven hundred residents, with units both for sale and for rent and a third of the total being 'affordable'. An element of 'live/work' spaces was included, together with community facilities such as a nursery and a health centre.

The basic module is that of a three-storey townhouse terrace, capable of being sliced up vertically into individual houses or cut up into flats and maisonettes. Every unit has access to a garden space, though many of these are formed as planted balconies or roof gardens and in some cases are accessible only via bridge links. Residential units face south to benefit from sunlight, workspaces north.

BedZED is visually arresting, with brightly coloured wind cowls as an eye-catcher and a pleasing materials mix of brick and untreated oak boarding; it stands out a mile from the routine speculative housing schemes in the vicinity. Internally, it offers generous spaces a cut above the typical developer product. But the point of the place is not how it looks but how it performs in environmental terms. The agenda was determinedly eco-friendly, beginning with the choice of site, continuing with the commitment to use recycled and low-energy materials for construction, and culminating in a services programme that reduces energy consumption by 60% in comparison to the typical family home; it is claimed there are virtually zero carbon emissions. These results are obtained by common-sense solutions that, alas, have been largely ignored by volume house builders: good insulation (thick walls and concrete floor slabs), the controlled use of the sun's light and warmth (with glazed sun-spaces to act as environmental buffers), natural ventilation (hence the rooftop cowls, which incorporate heat exchangers) and a combined heat and power plant, serving the whole complex, that can burn waste materials. Rainwater and waste water are recycled for reuse site. The development attracted keen interest from prospective residents long before completion and has generated a community that appears to love the lifestyle that It supports.

Opposite
Built of locally sourced and partly recycled components, the development is set in a traffic-free landscape.

Left
Colourful wind cowls, designed to catch the wind and push it through the buildings, form a marker for this innovative housing development.

BRICK LEAF HOUSE, HAMPSTEAD, NW3

WOOLF ARCHITECTS, 2000–03

Described by the RIBA Awards group – the project was an award winner in 2004 – as "perhaps the most luxurious back to back houses ever built", these linked houses on the edge of Hampstead Heath were commissioned by two brothers who are in business together and wished to live and work on the same site. The first complete building by Jonathan Woolf's youthful practice, the pair of houses (built on the site of a demolished 1970s house) was the subject of a competition, with the clients initially seeking a "white modern" aesthetic. They were persuaded by the architect to opt for handmade brick; as a result, the houses, though uncompromisingly contemporary, seem as much at ease in their green context as the more traditional residences in the vicinity.

The project, indeed, makes a very strong response to its setting, with several magnificent mature trees as defining features in the steeply sloping garden. The houses are designed to capitalize on immediate and more distant views out: from the heights of the heath there is a fine prospect of central London. The idea of a 'double house' is not new – Alexander 'Greek' Thomson designed a famous example in Glasgow – but in this instance the houses are linked not only as a single architectural composition, but also operationally. The two families share the garden and the basement pool and gym, and the clients' office is located in the garden. In other respects, though the houses have a common diagram, focused on double-height, top-lit atria that flood their interiors with benign natural light, each house has a distinct character. This derives not only from the personal taste of the respective occupants, in terms of décor and furnishings, but also from the disposition of each on the sloping site. Both houses are entered from the north, where a granite sett drive provides access for pedestrians and vehicles. From this point, their internal layouts are defined by the contours of the site: in the west house, for example, the internal spaces step down from the entrance. This house looks out to a splendid old oak tree set in an intimate enclosed garden area. The east house, in contrast, focuses on a fine copper beech with the office/studio annexe beyond. All the principal rooms in both houses are designed to address the garden.

Internally, the emphasis is on comfort and liveability rather than spatial effects. Only the subterranean pool astonishes, not least for the way in which natural light is channelled down to dramatize the space. This is the one truly extravagant gesture in the project, which, though (at £2,300,000) beyond the pockets of most Londoners, has significance for the broad field of house design in the capital, not least for its revisiting of the themes of community and privacy that preoccupied progressive housing design forty or more years ago.

COOKSON SMITH HOUSE, TWICKENHAM
EDWARD CULLINAN ARCHITECTS, 1999–2000

Opposite
Skilful use has been made of a relatively narrow site, with stepped pavilions extending from road to riverbank.

Below
Externally faced in natural materials – in particular brick and timber – the house has a spectacular internal living space that looks out on to the river.

The Cullinan office has designed remarkably few private houses, unsurprisingly, perhaps, given its strong commitment to social and public architecture. The exceptions are the houses built by the members of the practice for themselves, including Ted Cullinan's own residence, self-built "during two years of Sundays between 1962 and 1964". The architect for whom this luxurious riverside pavilion was designed presumably has neither the time nor the inclination for self-building.

The key issue was clearly the relationship of the house to the river. The architects' first inclination was to capitalize on it by creating a series of pavilions along the full width of the plot, but this proposal foundered after planners insisted on a rigorous programme of tree preservation (mere sycamores, it should be said). Instead, the house assumed a superficially straightforward rectangular form; even so, a planning appeal was needed before consent was given. In fact, the block is still broken down into three linked pavilions arranged on a north–south axis, two of three storeys, one of two storeys, under gently curving roofs, oversailing at the edges. A similar treatment is applied to the detached garage (with service flat above) on the road front of the site, so that the rhythm of curves extends across the whole complex of structures, marking a progression from road to river, from public to private domain. A timber deck extends through the entrance lobby (covered by a curved canopy) right down to the river bank, terminating in what looks like a diving board.

The use of brick and red cedar as the principal facing materials allows the house to fit easily into the local scene. The interior contains some surprises: a great full-height curving wall runs right through it, linking the spaces. It is punctuated by a series of openings and niches, elements in the rich texture of a house that the critic Jonathan Hale thought "more John Soane than John Pawson – and, I imagine, all the more liveable for it".

DIRTY HOUSE, WHITECHAPEL, E1

ADJAYE ASSOCIATES, 2001–02

Opposite
The Dirty House presents an enigmatic, even anonymous, façade to the East End street in which it stands.

Below
The interior makes skilful use of toplighting, while an external terrace offers views across the City of London.

David Adjaye's Elektra House in Whitechapel, east London (see p. 162), completed in 2000, created something of a furore: its entirely blank street façade was criticized as an antisocial, defensive gesture. But the form of the house was both a response to a deprived area and a reflection of the needs of the occupants.

The enigmatically named Dirty House, located in the same area, is an equally unsettling design, eschewing conventional notions of domestic ease. Like the Elektra House it is intended as a live/work space (for artists Tim Noble and Sue Webster). The house is basically a conversion of a plain 1930s warehouse. The internal structure was removed, in consultation with engineer Techniker, to make two double-height studios that occupy most of the ground and first floors. A new residential pavilion, fully glazed, sits on the roof, its own roof cantilevering out to cover an external terrace; lighting fitted under the timber decking makes this part of the building appear as a dramatic light beam by night. The setting back of the pavilion ensures complete privacy. The main street façades have been covered in anti-graffiti paint and fitted with double-glazed mirror-glass windows, so that from the outside the house appears impenetrable and disturbingly anonymous. There is an air of menace, too, in the very narrow, two-storey-high hallway through which the house is entered.

Like John Soane, Adjaye uses architectural form to create strong emotional responses: his is an architecture of sensation rather than conventional aesthetics, and compression is a device he uses to powerful effect. Adjaye's skilful use of toplighting is equally Soanean. However, as a modern architect for whom Soane's Classical inheritance is meaningless, Adjaye eschews elaborate detail in favour of a virtuoso approach to the use of materials – whether costly or, like those in this house, essentially commonplace.

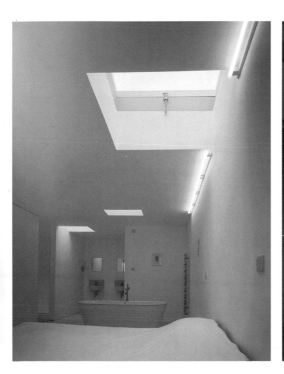

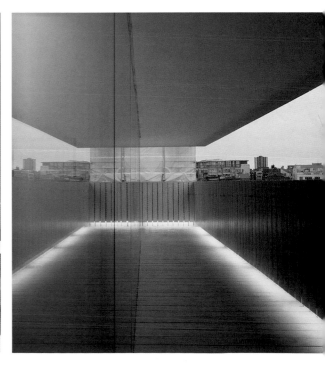

ELEKTRA HOUSE, WHITECHAPEL, E1

ADJAYE ASSOCIATES, 1999–2000

This is one of the most sensational new houses in London, a building that has the same power to shock and to annoy as the work of some of the artists for whom Adjaye, a new-generation star, has designed homes and studios. Its publication in an architectural journal produced much splenetic comment. Not the least of the charges laid against it was that its response to the street was hostile, defensive and anti-social, while exception was taken to its use as a family home.

Two artists were the clients for the Elektra House, located in a gritty but fashionable quarter of the East End. The decision to light the house entirely from above and from the rear, courtyard elevation was partly practical (for security and to obtain large interior wall surfaces for displaying art works) and partly the arbitrary decision of a designer who likes to do the unexpected. The street façade is clad in panels of black resin-coated plywood and is uncompromised by any openings; the entrance is via a passage to the side. Inside, the house is painted all white. The ground floor is almost entirely taken up by a studio/living room that opens into a small walled yard. A double-height slot illuminates the space and the staircase. The first floor contains three bedrooms and a bathroom, all largely dependent on roof lights for illumination and uncommonly tall in proportion.

This is an uncompromising statement of a house, tailor-made for the lifestyle of a particular family. Neither the street in which it stands nor London has been impoverished by it. Rather the opposite: it is a statement about the right of architect and client to work together to create something remarkable; London is being wrecked by house builders who create a standard product without reference to future users. In case the Elektra House should be considered an extravagant project, its cost should be put on record: £80,000 for 130 square metres of space, exclusive of site and fees.

Below
If the street façade, clad in black resin-coated plywood panels, is regarded by some as perversely blank, the rear is altogether lighter in tone and heavily glazed, offering views on to a small courtyard garden.

GARNER STREET HOUSE
BETHNAL GREEN, E2

FAT, 2000–02

FAT (standing for Fashion, Architecture and Taste) is a design collaborative accustomed to infringing the rules of 'good' taste, so you would expect a house designed by partner Sean Griffiths for his own occupation to be anything but conventional. In fact, Griffiths's house at Garner Street, Bethnal Green, is deliberately populist and pop, designed to communicate with the surrounding community. It opens up to the gritty streets of the East End as if they were located in some gentrified seaport in New England.

The American theme is to the fore here. American Postmodernism has always generated hostility in Britain, being seen as reactionary, trite and lacking in seriousness, and the work of Robert Venturi (responsible for the admittedly lacklustre Sainsbury Wing at The National Gallery, London) has been singled out for special condemnation. Venturi's work is the first comparison that springs to mind when you see the extraordinary street elevation of the Garner Street House. This consists of a cut-out house front, complete with chimney and garden hedge, standing in front of a cut-out office-block façade. Along the side elevation the roofline is decorated with cut-out gables imitating those in Amsterdam. The whole edifice is clad in clapboard, painted sky blue.

The plan of the house too owes something to Venturi/Scott Brown, with a staircase that wraps around the front of the house, creating a double façade, and embraces the kitchen inglenook. Griffiths, however, describes his creation as "Adolf Loos meets South Park ... . It is deliberately cartoon-like and representational in appearance and its 'pop' references seek to communicate with a wide audience."

The house includes both an office area and a separate top-floor flat, both accessed directly from the street. The house itself is entered from the yard at the side. The kitchen/dining-room is the heart of the house, with bedrooms on two floors above. Apart from Anglo-American PoMo and Pop, the pervasive influence seems to be that of the Arts and Crafts Movement: some of the detail refers explicitly to the Arts and Crafts architect and designer Charles Voysey. Strong colours are used throughout. All in all, it is hugely out of step with its environs. Griffiths denies that the house is in any way flippant, yet its obvious wit and lack of guile are attractive. This is one of the oddest and most memorable London houses since Piers Gough's residence, completed in 1988, for the journalist Janet Street-Porter in Clerkenwell, London.

Left
FAT's Garner Street House externally makes obvious reference to the pop imagery of Postmodernism (top), but internally combines free-flowing contemporary space with Art and Crafts-inspired details (middle and bottom).

HOUSE, 125 GOLDEN LANE, EC1
USE ARCHITECTS (JO HAGAN), 1999–2000

An oddity and a gem: a house just 3.5 metres wide slotted into the densely developed urban fabric of Clerkenwell and making a distinctive contribution to a townscape that includes Chamberlin, Powell & Bon's Golden Lane Estate and the spectacular towers of the same firm's Barbican development.

Hagan acquired the site when it housed nothing more than a shed, used by a mini-cab firm, squeezed into the gap between a Victorian commercial block and a pub. He intended to build a house for himself but ended up completing the project for a client, a couple with a young child. Negotiating with adjacent owners was one of the hardest parts of the project: inserting 13-metre piles meant working next to party walls. The plan emerges from the site: there was space for just one room per floor. The house has five floors, plus a basement and a small top floor space in a set-back behind

a roof terrace. The client's decision that a lift was a vital addition to the original proposals further restricted the internal space. The lift was inserted as a concrete shaft into a lightweight, steel-framed structure and is seen as a freestanding object. To the street, the house is a sheer composition of steel and glass, like a fragment of some large Mies tower, and the detailing is sufficiently precise to bear out the illusion. On the exposed side wall, timber cladding has been used, with a cut-out to allow views from the roof.

Five-storey houses are common enough in London, a vertical city. In many Georgian houses, staircases form the *tour de force*, and Hagan has worked within this tradition, making the stair a huge lightwell with views both inwards and outwards. The total cost of the project was £425,000 – reasonable for a house that is likely to remain a one-off.

Right and opposite
Highly vertical in the London tradition, and a rare example of an entirely new house close to the centre of the City, this project makes daring use of an alarmingly narrow site.

HOUSE, 180 HIGHBURY HILL, N5

CHARLES THOMSON/RIVINGTON STREET STUDIO, 1999–2000

Close to Arsenal's Highbury ground and Arsenal tube station, in an area of modest Victorian terraced houses, a new house utilizes a typical piece of urban waste ground formerly occupied by a derelict workshop. The aim was to design a classic modern house without concessions to history but in sympathy with the neighbourhood – 'modern, but contextual' is the formula. The relationship of the new building to the street and the way in which its response to the public domain was balanced by issues of seclusion and privacy were part of a dialogue with planners.

On the street front, the house maintains the two-storey scale of its neighbours, rising to three storeys at the rear. The designs seek to reinterpret the traditional formula of the London terraced house in a contemporary way. The roof is of zinc, rather than slate or tiles, the walls are white, sealed with an acrylic finish that eliminates the need for cavities and internal insulation. The steel-framed windows are slim and precise and adapted in form to their location: large bay windows on the street provide generous light and views out; on the rear elevation, long horizontal windows are more modern.

The plan is far from traditional, with a large L-shaped living room as the principal space, opening on to a garden deck. A further living/dining space occupies much of the first floor. Ceiling heights throughout are uncommonly generous by modern standards; indeed, the dimensions feel Victorian rather than modern.

Opposite
This house is uncompromisingly modern, while respectful of its Victorian neighbours.

Right and below
Inside, the use of light is modulated through narrow fenestration, while the aesthetic is modernist in its restraint.

HOUSE, TITE STREET, SW3
TONY FRETTON ARCHITECTS, 1997–2001

Tony Fretton's Lisson Gallery, in Lisson Street, Marylebone, completed fifteen years ago, was a radical statement about the nature of an art gallery, in spatial and in urban terms: the Lisson is a gallery on the street, open in its nature, with apartments above the display spaces.

Fretton's Chelsea house, designed for a reclusive art collector, is equally an urban statement, imbued with the architect's subtle and austere approach to space and form. The context is a street where the dominant theme is the late Victorian Domestic Revival style: red brick, bays and bows, all 'sweetness and light' – potentially dangerous territory for anyone trying to build in a contemporary way. In this instance, Fretton needed all the subtlety at his command to overcome possible objections, yet the house, though a private domain, is anything but recessive or anonymous. Its street front, indeed, has a solid dignity that Fretton sees as "civic – like a Venetian palazzo. Contributing to the city without being open to the public." The comparison is borne out by the plan

of the house, with a grand saloon at first floor level (*piano nobile*), extending into a void on the second floor, where there is a library. The spaces on these floors are intended for entertaining and the display of works of art. The house includes a small enclosed garden at the rear. It is, of course, an artistic house in the best Chelsea tradition: one recalls Whistler's house in Tite Street, designed by E.W. Godwin and proto-modern in its austerity.

Godwin's protest against convention lay in the use of white paint. Fretton is more contextual: the red limestone (an opulent choice of material) in which the house is clad is hardly an outrage in a street of red brick. But the precision with which it is used is more Miesian than Arts and Crafts. The house could be seen as over-monumental – a display of wealth – and defensive. But Fretton's references to Renaissance palazzi make sense. This house enriches the street. What goes on inside is the business of the owner – but one longs to see the interiors.

Right
The rigour and monumentality of this house provide a sensitive contrast with the more ornamental façades of its largely Victorian neighbours.

The generous scale of the house is equally reflected in the interiors, intended for the display of artworks.

Opposite
At the rear, a small enclosed garden can be enjoyed as much from inside as out.

HOUSING, COIN STREET, SE1

HAWORTH TOMPKINS ARCHITECTS, 1997–2001

This development of fifty-nine dwellings, including thirty-two family houses, by one of London's most dynamic young practices forms the latest segment in Coin Street Community Builders' ongoing development of the fourteen acres of land it acquired from the GLC in 1984 (purchase price: £1,000,000). The memory of the earliest work here – uninspired and suburban in character – has now been laid to rest as Coin Street moves on from the excellent mid-1990s contribution by Lifschutz Davidson (twenty-five units, including a nine-storey block) to this latest phase. Twenty years ago innovative design and social conviction seemed to be at odds, but this is no longer the case in Livingstone's London.

Haworth Tompkins won the commission in 1997. The site, formerly occupied by warehousing but used for surface parking for many years, is close to the National Theatre and high-rise IBM headquarters. The character of the new housing is suitably urban, mediating between the cultural/public territory of the South Bank and the modest residential streets beyond. There are four-storey houses on Coin Street and Cornwall Road. On Upper Ground, a busy public route through the area, the scale is even bigger, with two-storey maisonettes squatting on top of three-storey houses. Doors are on the street and houses have private gardens. Both the scale and the layout of the scheme (around a central square, with parking underneath) look back to Georgian tradition, though there is nothing overtly historicist about the architecture. On the street façades, a disciplined and impervious brick cladding is used. On the courtyard side, steel-and-timber balconies, with trellises and louvred-timber sun shades, create a softer, more lively and informal look. The materials have been used with a view to energy conservation. High levels of insulation and roof-mounted solar panels make the dwellings economical to run – this is sustainability in action.

The fourth side of the central square is to be occupied by the Hothouse, a new training centre with an IT resource centre, conference and classrooms, exhibition spaces, social facilities and small offices for local arts and community organizations. Facing the heavily trafficked Stamford Street, the building will provide a powerful image of genuinely creative community action to generate homes, employment and regeneration in partnership with business and government.

Opposite and top
The scheme proposes a new residential square –
a modern interpretation of an old London tradition.

Above
Faced in brick to the surrounding streets, the
housing blocks are more informal in appearance
on the elevations overlooking the new square,
and balconies, trellises and sunshading create
a lively aesthetic.

KEELING HOUSE REFURBISHMENT
CLAREDALE STREET, E2
MUNKENBECK & MARSHALL, 1999–2001

Munkenbeck & Marshall's revamp of Keeling House, Bethnal Green, as luxury apartments was welcomed by the original architect of the sixteen-storey block of maisonettes, the late Sir Denys Lasdun, though the project was at odds with the intentions behind his design. Built in 1957–59 for the borough council, Keeling House, like the slightly earlier 'cluster blocks' in Usk Street, represented a sincere attempt to create an environment where the community spirit of the East End might live on, even after the demolition of the traditional terraced streets of the area. The balconies, for example, were intended to encourage neighbourly chats.

Keeling House was emptied of tenants in 1992, when its allegedly poor structural condition began to give cause for alarm. Efforts to fund a refurbishment by a housing association failed and in 1999 the building, by then utterly derelict, was sold to a private developer. Saved from possible demolition by Grade II* listing, it had acquired the status of a modern classic.

The refurbishment project highlighted the relatively sound condition of the block: the concrete, in generally good condition, was sealed with a new protective coating. Original colours were reinstated throughout. In tune with the expectations of the new owner-occupiers, the setting of the building was enhanced and landscaped, with extensive planting and a pool within a secure enclosure. Lasdun and his former partner John Hurley collaborated on the design of a new entrance lobby, its triangular geometry derived from the form of the building.

Lasdun, who felt that gentrification was preferable to demolition, was equally supportive of a proposal to build a new penthouse on top of the block, but this was vetoed after a public inquiry in 2001, when a tablet in his memory was unveiled in the entrance lobby.

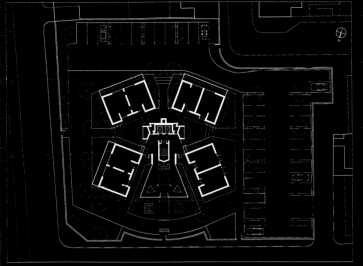

Opposite
A new entrance lobby was added to the existing building as part of its conversion.

Left
The form of Sir Denys Lasdun's original cluster blocks has adapted well to the lifestyle of a social group far removed from the original inhabitants of the scheme.

The development includes new landscaping of the area around the building, and secure car parking.

KNIGHT HOUSE, RICHMOND UPON THAMES, SURREY

DAVID CHIPPERFIELD ARCHITECTS, 1987–90; EXTENDED 2001

To the existing 1980s house (below, left and right), David Chipperfield has added a new pavilion (below, middle, and opposite) that contains an office with a bedroom above. The glazed end wall of the bedroom slides down to form an open loggia.

When Chipperfield designed the house at Richmond for Nick and Charlotte Knight he was known for domestic work and shop interiors. Twenty years on, and he has behind him large-scale public commissions in Germany, Spain and Italy, as well as a substantial project in Britain (BBC Scotland, Pacific Quay, Glasgow).

The original Knight House was, in theory, an enlargement and reworking of an existing house set in a typical suburban avenue. In fact, the house was completely transformed so that it was more than doubled in size. The new house, which was highly contentious when built, extends into the rear garden, where a studio space overlooks a courtyard, itself enclosed by a concrete arch. One of its special strengths was the remarkable interaction of internal and external space, with a virtuosity in the management of natural light for which Chipperfield is now renowned. In many respects, this relatively modest house was one of the key British buildings of the 1980s. The 2001 extension was constructed on the site of a neighbouring house, acquired by the Knights and demolished. With its pitched, slate-covered roof (demanded by planners), it has an identity of its own, in tune with the ingrained individualism of the suburbs (where every plot is a separate domain). The extension provides an office and archive store at ground level, with a large bedroom above. A small link block, containing cloakrooms and a bathroom, connects new and existing elements; a small courtyard is formed between the two.

The diagram of the extension is as incisive and perfectly judged as you would expect from Chipperfield. The use of materials equally reflects the touch of a master. The beautifully constructed timber stair connecting the two floors is an exquisite thing in itself. Chipperfield's architecture is sometimes seen as a matter of control and refinement, but he enjoys dramatic gestures. The glazed end wall of the Knights' bedroom slides down into a slot in the floor, turning the whole room into an open loggia. The Knight House reflects admirably that quality described by one Italian critic as *un sensibile minimalismo*.

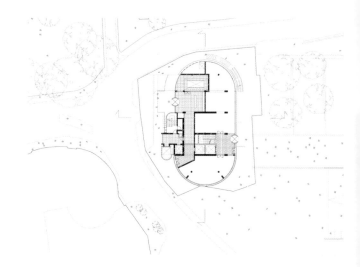

LONDON TOWN: 44 HOPTON STREET, SE1

KEVIN DASH ARCHITECTS/GUMUCHDJIAN ASSOCIATES, 1999–

The Cesar Pelli-designed residential tower adjacent to the Museum of Modern Art, New York, is one of the most desirable addresses in Manhattan. Philip Gumuchdjian and Kevin Dash's original, thirty-two-storey, 107-metre tall tower project for a site close to Tate Modern offered London its own version of the MOMA tower. Kevin Dash and Philip Gumuchdjian's scheme, designed for developer London Town plc, attracted the support of Mayor Livingstone, whose vision of a booming capitalist economy fuelling social progress it so vividly reflected.

The site was that of a paper warehouse, a shabby relic of the industries that once dominated Bankside. The footprint of the new tower (a little higher than Tate's chimney stack) would have occupied only a small part of the site, opening up the route to the Tate from Southwark station and Blackfriars Bridge. The slender form of the tower reduced the visual impact of the development and minimized both shadowing and potential wind turbulence.

The thirty-three apartments in the tower varied in size; the grandest would have been two-storey penthouses with some of the best views in London. A low-energy services programme included the use of timber louvres on the south and south-west façades, with automatic sunshading, chilled soffits (rather than conventional air conditioning), and provision of double-height winter gardens to provide an intermediate climatic zone. Shops and restaurants were planned at basement, ground- and first-floor levels.

The project won support from Southwark planners, but was rejected by the borough's planning committee. After a public inquiry in 2002, planning consent was finally secured but the scheme was the subject of a determined campaign by local residents and by Tate Director Sir Nicholas Serota, who argued that it was as bad as if a high-rise building were to be constructed in the forecourt of the British Museum. (This argument ignored the fact that part of the rationale for Tate Modern, an obsolete power station which had long been derided as an eyesore, was to regenerate the rundown riverside; 44 Hopton Street could be seen as a classic regenerative project.) A series of legal challenges to the planning consent followed, culminating in a House of Lords decision that it should stand. In 2005 there was the prospect of a possible appeal to the European Court of Human Rights which, if successful, would pose a challenge to the entire planning system. What is currently proposed is a twenty-storey tower, a trifle broader in the beam than the original proposal and with fewer housing units. This remains a good scheme, and it is hard to see the point of the extended campaign to stop it being built.

Above, below and opposite
The subject of a protracted planning battle, the Hopton Street tower, close to Tate Modern, will form a slender glassy presence on the riverside scene.

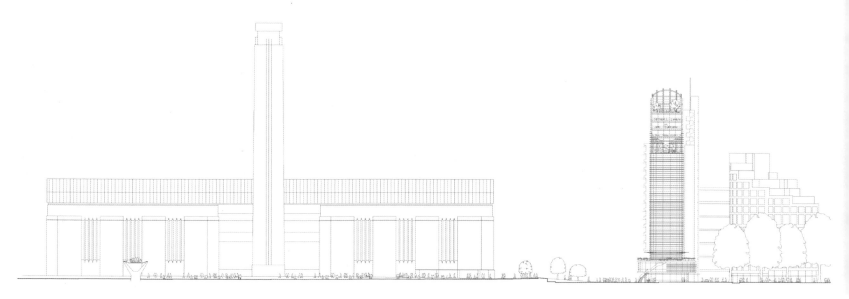

MILLENNIUM VILLAGE HOUSING
GREENWICH, SE10

ERSKINE TOVATT/EPR; PROCTOR MATTHEWS ARCHITECTS,

1997–

Below and opposite
With their flexible plans, double-height spaces, use of prefabricated components and strong colour, the houses at the Millennium Village provide a striking contrast to those typically offered by developers.

The 1997 competition for the development of the Millennium Village, a key element in the regeneration of the derelict and polluted Greenwich Peninsula, was won by Greenwich Millennium Village Ltd, working with the veteran Anglo-Swedish architect Ralph Erskine (in the context of a Richard Rogers masterplan for the peninsula). The designs have been developed and carried through to construction by Erskine's office in collaboration with the British EPR practice. One of the neighbourhoods in the village, with 189 housing units, was designed by the Proctor Matthews practice, again in tune with the masterplan, while a school and health centre there is the work of Edward Cullinan Architects.

The ongoing development of the area (long occupied by a vast gasworks) as a socially mixed neighbourhood was given a huge boost by the opening of the Jubilee Line station at North Greenwich, adjacent to Rogers's Millennium Dome (now planned to be recycled as a casino). Negative media coverage of the Dome has deflected attention from the long-term benefits of the Millennium Festival held there in 2000.

Erskine, best known in Britain for the innovative 'Byker Wall' housing of the 1970s in Newcastle-upon-Tyne, sought to imbue the new village with something of the sense of place and identity found in traditional urban settlements. He wants to create communities, not just areas of housing, and his architecture is flexible and unprescriptive in spirit. The village contains a mix of uses and social classes: 'affordable' housing is scattered throughout the scheme. A few years on, the vision is beginning to emerge as something more than wishful thinking. The masterplan, with its green

'eco-park' and central oval with retail and office development, is well considered. The housing itself is strong in form (and makes bold use of colour), but is tough and unprecious enough to survive the attentions of project managers and contractors and to lend itself to the use of prefabricated components. Within the overall framework there is scope for a number of housing types. Devices such as balconies, bays and varied claddings break down the uniformity of the blocks, which are tallest at the north-east edge of the site, close to the River Thames. High environmental standards are fundamental to the project: grey water is recycled and rainwater collected. Recycled materials have been extensively used and insulation values are high.

Proctor Matthews's housing responds wholeheartedly to the social commitment of Erskine's plan. It includes both apartment blocks of four to eight storeys and two- and three-storey houses, all crisply detailed; the aesthetic has an overall industrial and metallic feel. This is tempered, however, by the use of vivid colour and natural materials. But it is the interiors of these houses that demonstrate most clearly a determination to erode the barriers between social housing and that produced by the commercial market. Full-height windows, flexible plans, double-height spaces and third storeys on some of the houses are features that are not found in the 'social' housing of the recent past. Landscaping by Robert Rummey complements the exceptional quality of this development. The millennium has passed, but the Millennium Village is an optimistic place that seems to have avoided many of the mistakes that blighted earlier developments in Docklands.

Opposite
The Murray Grove housing was constructed to a tight schedule using prefabricated components.

Below
The five-storey building, with apartments accessed by external galleries, has a scale and urban character appropriate to its setting.

PEABODY HOUSING, MURRAY GROVE, N1
CARTWRIGHT PICKARD ARCHITECTS, 1998–99

Under the leadership of its development director Dickon Robinson, the Peabody Trust (established in 1862 and owner of 20,000 rented homes in London) has emerged as a highly innovative patron of new architecture, seeking to address the continuing shortage of affordable housing and the constantly changing lifestyles of Londoners, which have created a demand for something more than the typical 'family home'. Bill Dunster, CZWG and Allford Hall Monaghan Morris are among the practices commissioned by Peabody in the last few years. Robinson is a strong advocate of

increased density: Peabody is currently promoting the construction of a number of residential towers in London.

The housing at Murray Grove, completed in 1999, has a special interest in that the L-shaped, five-storey, thirty-apartment building, on the corner of Murray Grove and Shepherdess Walk, was constructed in only twenty-seven weeks (February–August 1999) using prefabricated modules. The development is arranged in two wings overlooking a landscaped courtyard.

The construction system is as straightforward as a set of toy bricks:

the modules, with plumbing, electrics, doors and windows already attached, are put together to form one-bed (two-module) and two-bed (three-module) units. Access is via external galleries along the street frontages, with bathrooms and kitchens placed here to baffle the street noise. On the garden side, overlooked by living and sleeping spaces, each flat has a balcony, large enough to accommodate a dining table: the "industrious artisans" whom Peabody originally set out to house have become sophisticated, though relatively impecunious nurses, teachers and the like.

Murray Grove continues to attract interest as an example of quality housing procured to a fast-track schedule (though the turn-out cost was eventually some 15% more than had been targeted). It is also a very decent piece of urban architecture, well related to the street, with terracotta facing used to reflect the red-brick aesthetic of nearby warehouses, and a strongly expressed lift/staircase tower marking the corner in typically London fashion. As starter homes for young 'key workers', the apartments here set a new standard.

PRIORY HEIGHTS, PRIORY GREEN ESTATE, N1
AVANTI ARCHITECTS, 1998–2000

At first glance, Priory Heights (formerly Wynford House) looks much like hundreds of other local authority housing blocks in London. Closer study of form and details reveals, however, the touch of a master, in this case Berthold Lubetkin, a Modern Movement pioneer whose impact on London was enormous. In the post-war years Lubetkin built on the social promise of the Finsbury Health Centre and moved boldly into the field of housing. The Priory Green Estate was begun in 1948, though Wynford House was not started until 1954, as part of a second phase of development, and completed only in 1957, long after the dissolution of Tecton. It was always intended as a one-off block, though some of the design refinements proposed (internal access by lifts, for example, and private balconies) were omitted on grounds of cost. As usual, it was a matter of false economy, contributing to the downgrading of the estate in more recent years, when extensive demolition was seriously contemplated.

Avanti's refurbishment of Priory Heights has emerged as the marker for an ongoing improvement programme for the entire estate. The block was sold by Islington Council to Community Housing Association in 1997, with Avanti – led by Lubetkin's biographer, John Allan – in charge of the reconstruction project. The block has been reconfigured on the basis of mixed tenure to provide sixty-two private rented units and twenty-six social housing units, this formula generated sufficient revenue to finance a high-quality scheme. Ailing concrete has been restored where necessary, without recourse to crude overcladding, and original finishes and colours have been reinstated. The services, including the lift system, have been comprehensively upgraded. Modern standards of energy efficiency demanded the replacement of the original metal windows, though their substitutes look identical. On top of the building, plant and water-tank installations have been converted into stunning penthouses, with views across London. The project was completed in spring 2000, and all the units were quickly let. Hugely stylish, the project demonstrates one way ahead for London's sometimes problematic stock of post-1945 social housing.

Opposite and left
The Priory Heights project symbolizes huge potential for refurbishing and recycling allegedly obsolete public housing and has spearheaded a regeneration campaign for the estate in which the block stands.

10–22 SHEPHERDESS WALK, N1

BUSCHOW HENLEY, 1997–99

A landmark development on the modish border of Shoreditch and Hackney, epicentre of the London art and design world at the beginning of the twenty-first century, Buschow Henley's conversion of a former warehouse in Shepherdess Walk gives definition to the somewhat nebulous concept of the 'loft'.

The raw material was good: a solidly constructed 10,200-square-metre building in two main blocks of five and six storeys around a long central yard. It was opportune, perhaps, that the budget was quite tight. According to the architects, the aims of the project were "pragmatic, reconfiguring the plan, restructuring the building, a series of interconnecting decisions were to subvert the usual order ... there was not to be an idealized conception".

A particular feature of the building was its division by load-bearing walls into a series of vertical 'tenements', each with its own entrance from the street.

The aim was a mixed-use development: the ground floor is allocated for commercial use, with fifty dual-aspect apartments upstairs. The decision to retain the structural form of the building produced apartments of an L shape – not inconvenient, since it generated an alternative to the conventional (and intrusive) free-standing service core.

The verve with which this project was driven forward by developer and architect is reflected in the treatment of the courtyard as a generous communal space (the new lift tower is the most prominent addition) and even more in the extraordinary roofscape. With the original proposal of an additional, glazed top floor rejected by planners, a new rooftop scene of detached pavilions, clad in zinc (like the typical Hoxton bar-top), was created. Some of the pavilions have gardens attached – this is "suburbia on the roof". The ad hoc, cumulative approach is in a London, not to say Cockney, tradition: one thinks of the typical East End allotment. Buschow Henley has captured the essence of loft living at Shepherdess Walk, with a building that carries the potential for further change and adaptation. This is practical conservation at its best.

Below, left and middle
The project recycled a former warehouse in Shoreditch as a mixed-use development in which the flat roof of the building was colonized with new pavilions and gardens.

Below, right and opposite
The focus of the scheme is the central courtyard, a communal space overlooked by access galleries and punctuated by the new glazed lift tower.

STRAW HOUSE AND QUILTED OFFICE
STOCK ORCHARD STREET, N7

SARAH WIGGLESWORTH ARCHITECTS/JEREMY TILL,
1999–2001

Standing hard up against the main railway line into King's Cross, Wigglesworth and Till's Straw House is probably the most-discussed London private house since Future Systems' all-glass Hauer/King House of 1994. The architects wanted a house for their own occupation, plus a professional studio office. The project was seen as a clear demonstration of the principles of sustainability and low-energy design, a potential exemplar for the housing market more generally, rather than an eccentric excursion into the merely avant-garde. At the same time, it has created a beguilingly quiet oasis in the inner-city, a surprisingly calm place for living and working.

Anyone expecting a thatched cottage look is in for a surprise. Straw (barley, it is reported) is used, not in a traditional way, but as a cheap and effective means of insulation, stacked in the form of bales, to cocoon the bedroom wing of the house; inside, they are lime plastered. The main living level is raised above the ground, a place of light and flexible space, illuminated by a wall of protective glazing that filters the sunlight and reduces solar gain. The roof is covered in earth and planted with grass and wild flowers, with a five-floor book tower rising through it and providing a look-out reading room at the top. The office wing extends along the railway, with trains passing every few minutes, so that good acoustic insulation is vital and is provided by a thick layer of sand-filled sacks, raised up on gabions – metal cages filled with crushed waste concrete.

The sustainable credentials of the project are serious: even the book tower has an environmental function, acting as a thermal flue and ventilating the house. Rainwater is collected and used for watering and to supply lavatories and washing machines. The architects claim that their composting toilet is "one of the first to be used in the UK in an urban situation". But there is nothing hair-shirt about the house and studio: its ethos of delight in materials, combined with a sound moral end, seems, indeed, to recall the best aspects of the Arts and Crafts movement, redrawn in the light of twenty-first century issues.

Opposite and left
This live–work settlement in the inner city is a demonstration project in which the potential of sustainable design and low-energy materials is explored.

TALL HOUSE, ARTHUR ROAD
WIMBLEDON, SW19

TERRY PAWSON, 1996–2002

Houses designed by architects for themselves arguably form a genre in their own right, although it is interesting that many of the biggest names in British architecture – James Stirling, the Smithsons, Rogers and Foster, for example – have opted for adaptations of existing buildings as their London homes. One of the modern classics of London is, however, the elegant 1960s steel house near Wimbledon Common that Richard Rogers designed for his parents. Terry Pawson's house is about 1.5 kilometres away, in an avenue of prosperous Edwardian villas close to Wimbledon Park station.

While the Rogers house, case-study inspired, exemplifies the universalism of the High-tech tradition – it would be at home in Malibu – the Pawson house is more complex, a response to site and context and subtly inspired by history. Pawson cites the nineteenth-century English architect Sir John Soane as one of his greatest

inspirations; Soane's influence is reflected in the spatial qualities of the house and its skilful use of toplighting. Architects Louis Kahn and Tadao Ando are other influences, but all are comfortably subsumed into what is a mature and considered work.

The site of the house is extremely narrow and falls away steeply from the road. The section is the key. The principal living spaces are contained in a two-storey, barrel-vaulted concrete pavilion that steps down the slope to the garden. The bedrooms and bathrooms are placed in a four-storey tower, timber-framed (and timber-clad, using unseasoned oak) and facing the road. A full-height staircase hall, top-lit, connects these two elements and is an ideal space for the display of art works. The house is an assembly of pieces in the tradition of James Stirling. Its interior character is formed by contrasting textures: exposed concrete and finely crafted timber floors, and built-in furniture.

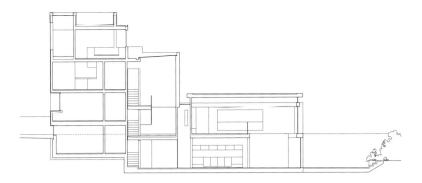

Opposite and top left
Bedrooms and bathrooms are placed in a four-storey tower – containing a dramatic, even perilous, staircase – facing the road.

Bottom left and above
The principal living spaces are housed in a low-rise wing to the rear, facing the garden.

VXO HOUSE, SPANIARDS END
HAMPSTEAD, NW3

ALISON BROOKS ARCHITECTS, 1999–2001

Alison Brooks's VXO House is basically a reworking of an unremarkable house of the 1960s. Hamfistedly extended during the 1970s – space was gained at the expense of convenience and legibility – it now forms the core of a remarkable residential complex in which wit and lightness of touch are the distinguishing themes.

The 1960s house (which was damaged by fire when Brooks was commissioned) stood in a generous garden in Hampstead, set back from the street behind an enclosing wall. The initial brief was one of repair, conversion and extension, with an extra bedroom and a more generous entrance space to be provided. The project subsequently grew to include a radical reconstruction of the existing house, new structures in the garden and a reconfiguration of the landscape. The architect describes the completed project as "a domestic campus of enclosed, semi-enclosed and open structures". The changes are far from cosmetic and exhibit, for a relatively modest project costing under £600,000, a considerable element of structural bravura by the consultant engineers Price & Myers.

The additional space to the existing house could only be provided on the garden front, where it is conceived as a timber-clad volume hovering over a new glazed terrace and supported on a single 'V' column, painted bright red. Inside, a new suspended staircase, contained within steel mesh, is hung from the first floor within a new central atrium, which is the focus of the house. A free-standing screen wall, the work of artist Simon Patterson, conceals the cloakroom, and a new dining-room has been created where there was formerly an outdoor terrace. New timber decks connect internal and external spaces.

The separate X-pavilion (replacing a double garage and containing a gym and guest accommodation) is conceived as a pure glass box, sitting on a folded *in situ* concrete plate that provides the base for the building and a retaining wall. Inside, a folded timber plate forms both a floor and a screen wall. The earth-covered roof of the pavilion is carried on two 'X' members.

Finally, the existing car port has been replaced by a new 'O port' – just a roof, dramatically cantilevered, sitting on a light steel structure of which the 'O' forms part. Inside the house, high-quality materials, including aluminium, choice woods, etched glass and limestone, are used freely. The essence of the project seems to be the attempt to erode the barriers between the highly tactile interior and the openness of the garden beyond.

Right and opposite
The VXO project – the initials of which are derived from the boldly painted steel structural members – includes the refurbishment of an existing house, the construction of a new glazed pavilion containing gym and guest accommodation, and a new car port. The three buildings form a family of structures within the context of the lushly planted garden.

ALLIES & MORRISON STUDIOS
ALLIES & MORRISON

BANKSIDE 123
ALLIES & MORRISON

BENNETTS ASSOCIATES LONDON OFFICE
BENNETTS ASSOCIATES

110 BISHOPSGATE
KOHN PEDERSEN FOX

BROADWICK HOUSE, BROADWICK STREET
RICHARD ROGERS PARTNERSHIP

CHISWICK PARK
RICHARD ROGERS PARTNERSHIP

CITY HALL
FOSTER AND PARTNERS

J.C. DECAUX HEADQUARTERS
FOSTER AND PARTNERS

27–30 FINSBURY SQUARE
ERIC PARRY ARCHITECTS

HABERDASHERS' HALL
MICHAEL HOPKINS & PARTNERS

HOME OFFICE AND HM PRISON SERVICE HEADQUARTERS
TERRY FARRELL & PARTNERS

LLOYD'S REGISTER OF SHIPPING
RICHARD ROGERS PARTNERSHIP

LONDON BRIDGE TOWER
RENZO PIANO BUILDING WORKSHOP/BROADWAY MALYAN

MERRILL LYNCH FINANCIAL CENTRE
SWANKE HAYDEN CONNELL ARCHITECTS

THE MINERVA BUILDING
NICHOLAS GRIMSHAW & PARTNERS

PADDINGTON BASIN
TERRY FARRELL & PARTNERS/RICHARD ROGERS PARTNERSHIP

PALESTRA, BLACKFRIARS ROAD
ALSOP ARCHITECTS

PATERNOSTER SQUARE
WHITFIELD PARTNERS (MASTERPLAN)/ALLIES & MORRISON/
MacCORMAC JAMIESON PRICHARD/SIDELL GIBSON/ERIC PARRY
ARCHITECTS/SHEPPARD ROBSON

PORTCULLIS HOUSE (NEW PARLIAMENTARY BUILDING)
MICHAEL HOPKINS & PARTNERS

SWISS RE HEADQUARTERS
FOSTER AND PARTNERS

TALKBACK HEADQUARTERS, NEWMAN STREET
BUSCHOW HENLEY

WELLCOME TRUST HEADQUARTERS
HOPKINS ARCHITECTS

WINCHESTER HOUSE, LONDON WALL
SWANKE HAYDEN CONNELL

88 WOOD STREET
RICHARD ROGERS PARTNERSHIP

ALLIES & MORRISON STUDIOS
85 SOUTHWARK STREET, SE1

ALLIES & MORRISON, 2001–03

Below and opposite
Occupying an irregularly shaped site on Southwark Street, Allies & Morrison Studios incorporates landscaped spaces to the rear, while the main street façade is highly transparent and animated by bold use of colour.

Allies & Morrison's move to Southwark reflects both the remarkable growth of the practice (to more than 150 staff), necessitating a move from increasingly cramped offices in W1, and the rise of SE1 as a stylish business address. A site for the firm's new building was secured on Southwark Street, directly opposite the Bankside 123 development (Allies & Morrison's biggest job to date; see pp. 196–97) and a short walk from Tate Modern.

The building makes a positive addition to Southwark Street, which can seem a monotonous thoroughfare, by day and by night. The street elevation (which faces north) is fully glazed and elegantly detailed, with brightly coloured internal shutters to deflect sunlight when necessary or simply to secure privacy. Its transparency is a relief in the context of the heavyweight brick facades of adjacent warehouses, and

it is a beacon of light and colour on a dark winter afternoon.

Internally, the building focuses on the stepped atrium, formed on the south side of the irregularly shaped site, which provides a visual and operational connection between the six storeys of office floors. The character of the interior is defined by the use of high-quality fair-faced concrete, left exposed throughout (there are no suspended ceilings and a virtual ban on plasterboard). The main staircase is a *tour de force*. Metalwork is finished to a heavy-duty industrial grade, and the floors are of black granite (in the ground-floor reception/ exhibition area) or grey resin. A roof garden, facing south, is an amenity in fine weather.

The ground-floor plan incorporates a through route from Southwark Street southwards, a recognition of the need to open links between the riverside and the hinterland.

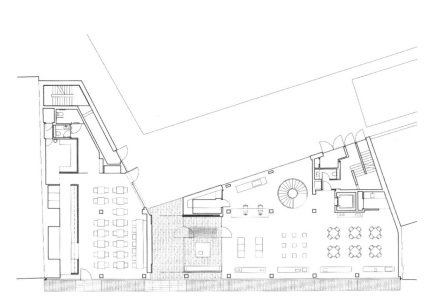

Bankside 123 is the largest project so far undertaken by Allies & Morrison, now acknowledged as one of London's most successful younger practices (it was established in the 1980s) and with its own stunning offices conveniently located directly opposite the Bankside 123 site (see pp. 194–95). The development replaces St Christopher House, allegedly "the largest office block under one roof in Europe" when completed in 1959 and a depressing habitat for the thousands of civil servants who occupied it up to the time of its sale and eventual demolition in 2003.

St Christopher House was a looming and impermeable presence, yet Allies & Morrison's project for developer Land Securities painlessly increases the amount of office space on the site, while providing much-needed new shopping for the area and – most significantly – creating public routes across the site to and from Tate Modern behind it.

The three new buildings, containing more than 102,190 square metres (gross) of office space and 9290 square metres of retailing, cafés and bars at street level, are arranged as city blocks penetrated by two pedestrian routes cut through the site, with two new public spaces at its eastern and western ends. The aim is to create a lively 'high street' frontage to Southwark Street, with shops and cafés opening off wide, tree-lined pavements. The buildings are conceived as a group but each is given a distinctive identity by the use of a wide palette of materials: metal and glass, terracotta and precast concrete. In contrast to the monolithic uniformity of St Christopher House, the new blocks are carefully massed in response to their context, with the scale of the scheme diminishing from west to east (where it abuts an area of housing).

Land Securities says that the success of the scheme depends as much on the quality of the overall environment it creates as on the design of the office buildings – hence its substantial investment in the public realm, in paving, planting, street furniture and artworks. The objective is a new business quarter, a further extension of the City in the mould of More London, complete with the amenities that attract the best staff, close to the cultural magnet of Tate Modern. The planned expansion of the latter will further reinforce the rationale of this approach. An associated residential development, designed by Richard Rogers Partnership and replacing low-value industrial sheds, is in the pipeline for an adjacent site.

Left and opposite
Though consisting mostly of office space, the Bankside 123 development includes substantial areas of public open space and provides new routes through from Tate Modern to the hinterland of Southwark.

BENNETTS ASSOCIATES LONDON OFFICE
RAWSTORNE PLACE, ISLINGTON, EC1

BENNETTS ASSOCIATES, 2001–02

The Islington offices of Bennetts Associates, the practice that Rab and Denise Bennetts founded in 1987, have the ambience more of a well-loved studio-cum-home than of a powerhouse of commercial design. Yet it is the growth of the practice, with a solid base of office commissions as well as such public works as the Gateway and Orientation Centre at Loch Lomond, that necessitated the move from its increasingly cramped base just 50 metres down the street.

The complex of buildings in Rawstorne Place, off St John Street, ranging in date from the eighteenth to the mid-twentieth centuries, was acquired as a result of a clear-out of surplus property by the local authority. It has been converted to house nearly fifty staff. The oldest element was an utterly derelict Georgian barn, once used by drovers taking cattle to Smithfield Market in east London. Historic buildings specialist Richard Griffiths advised on the rescue of this structure, which now houses two conference rooms and the practice library. It has been repaired as found, with rough brickwork and old timbers left exposed. A

new building wraps around the barn hard up against the rear-garden wall of a Victorian terrace; this contains the reception area and open-plan offices, partly in a lightweight mezzanine. It has a planted earth roof (providing excellent insulation) and is lit via a glazed clerestory. A minimal glazed link, containing a staircase, connects the barn to a former printworks, where there are two further floors of design studios, light and airy spaces overlooking the open courtyard.

Bennetts Associates has a reputation for pioneering sustainable design, and everything possible has been done to make this project environmentally responsible. Ventilation is entirely natural, materials found on site have been recycled, even the carpeting is made of recycled PVC. Recycling old buildings is, of course, one of the soundest ways of conserving scarce resources. This intelligent and highly practical mix of old and new provides the practice with an inspirational work space; it should inspire others to seek out the decaying interstices in the fabric of London.

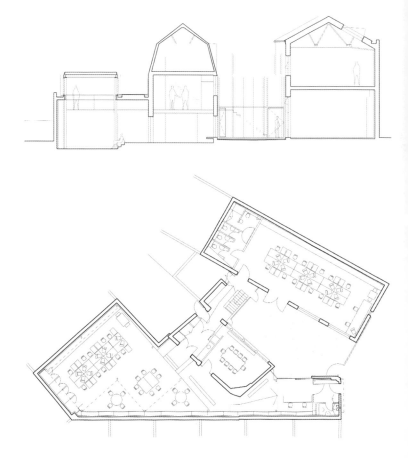

Above and opposite
The office complex fills an irregular site, which includes buildings that range in date from the eighteenth to the mid-twentieth centuries. The oldest element is a former barn, a remarkable survival that is now joined to a former printworks by a glazed link building. Around one side of the barn is a new reception area and additional office accommodation.

110 BISHOPSGATE, EC2

KOHN PEDERSEN FOX, 2000–

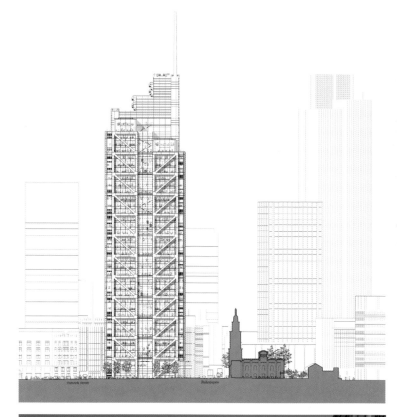

110 Bishopsgate – nicknamed Heron Tower after its developer – might appear a relatively uncontroversial project after Norman Foster's Swiss Re sailed through the planning process with backing from the City, English Heritage and the government. In spring 2001, however, a call-in order by Environment Secretary John Prescott stopped the scheme in its tracks and threw its future into question.

This is the second City project by Kohn Pedersen Fox, a practice originating in the United States but rapidly gaining serious credentials in Europe (Thames Court, Upper Thames Street, was finished in 1998). Another major office development by the practice has recently been completed just outside the City on High Holborn. Comparable in scale to Swiss Re and markedly less high than the 1970s Tower 42 (NatWest Tower), Kohn Pedersen Fox's building replaces a group of utterly banal 1970s buildings at Houndsditch, on the eastern boundary of the City. Far removed from the St Paul's Heights control zone, it would form part of a cluster of towers in this part of London, close to excellent public transport facilities. At street level the

scheme would produce real public benefits with part of Houndsditch closed to traffic and turned into a new square, framing the church of St Botolph. The lower levels of the building will be given over to shopping and restaurants, a public domain in marked contrast to the typically private City office lobby. There will be a public restaurant on top of the tower, a response to Mayor Ken Livingstone's call for high buildings to be accessible to all.

The aim has been to produce a highly transparent structure, light and elegant in form, and to instil seriously green ideas into the high building form. The south side of the tower, which faces a busy road, houses a concentration of services that baffle solar gain. On the north side, the building opens up to reveal the stacked three-storey atriums that serve a series of office 'villages'. The east and west façades are designed to provide natural ventilation for the office floors. Intended for multiple occupation by international businesses, the tower addresses the needs of the City as an international financial centre – and it would be a handsome addition to the skyline.

Right and opposite
Though smaller in scale than some recent or proposed additions to the London skyline, Kohn Pedersen Fox's Bishopsgate tower reflects a serious environmental and urban agenda, with façades designed to capitalize on natural light and ventilation, internal gardens and public amenities, including a new square and rooftop restaurant.

BROADWICK HOUSE
BROADWICK STREET, W1

RICHARD ROGERS PARTNERSHIP, 1996–2001

In contrast to other current Rogers projects, including Terminal 5, Heathrow, Chiswick Park and the office buildings at Paddington Basin, Broadwick House is, at 4000 square metres and a cost of under £7,000,000, small beer. However, the project underlines the fact that contextual architecture need not be faint-hearted stuff. The site is in the heart of Soho, at the corner of Broadwick Street and Berwick Street (where one of London's liveliest street markets takes place) and is an island, surrounded by streets and lanes. The new six-storey building, let to Ford Motor Company's design division, replaces an undistinguished post-war block. It is an exercise in good manners, though conducted within the framework of a bold approach to design.

The challenge in the scheme was to maximize accommodation on the footprint, while producing a building that is a good neighbour, at home in its surroundings. At street level, a generous set-back on the façades provides precious space for

pedestrians on the narrow and often crowded street. Ground floor and basement levels have been let to a restaurant, in tune with the existing character of Soho. The offices are entered via a triple aspect reception area on Broadwick Street, spanning the full width of the building. The most distinctive feature of the scheme is the stepping back of the offices at fifth and sixth floors beneath a great arched roof: the double-height top-floor offices have terrific views across the West End, with external terraces as extensions of the working spaces. Offices have floor-to-ceiling glazing, with screening to baffle the sun. A final touch of Rogers style is provided by the panoramic glazed lift tower, which focuses attention on the corner of the building and gives it a dynamic vertical thrust. The use of colour here and in the roof structure relieves an otherwise sombre palette of concrete, aluminium and stainless steel.

Right and opposite
Richard Rogers's Broadwick House is an example of uncompromising and expressive modern design in a historic context, with a finely detailed glazed lift tower forming a powerful marker on the corner of the building and injecting a new dynamism into the Soho street scene.

CHISWICK PARK, CHISWICK HIGH ROAD, W4
RICHARD ROGERS PARTNERSHIP, 1999–2003

Left and below
The completed buildings at Chiswick Park –
eleven blocks are planned, set in a lush
landscape – combine elegant form and
careful detailing with speed and economy
of construction and a progressive energy
strategy to make this the model business park
of the twenty-first century.

Chiswick Park is one of a number of major
London developments thrown into limbo by
the 1990s recession and subsequently
resurrected. The original masterplan was
prepared for Stanhope developers by Terry
Farrell. The thirty-three-acre site (formerly a
London Transport depot) was cleared and
some of the infrastructure carried out. Work
then stopped. The present project consists
of eleven buildings, all designed by Richard
Rogers, with up to 140,500 square metres
of space and a working population of ten

thousand. The phased construction
process began in 1999.

Stuart Lipton of Stanhope, still an
amazingly innovative figure on the London
development scene (and a longstanding
Rogers client), created the key business
park of the 1980s at Stockley Park, near
Heathrow. Chiswick Park is emerging as
something rather different. First, the diverse
architecture of Stockley (Skidmore, Owings
& Merrill, Arup, Foster, Eric Parry and
others) has given way to an overall look
that benefits from the advantages of
standardization. Secondly, although there
are parking spaces for 1700 cars, most
people working at Chiswick will travel there
by public transport, using two nearby
Underground stations. The new landscape
design by W8 provides for a greener and
more informal setting than that envisaged
by Farrell, with a sizeable park at the core of
the development. By placing parking in the
undercrofts of the buildings, Rogers avoids
the typical business-park look of isolated
blocks surrounded by lawns and cars.

The Rogers team has produced a
winning formula that combines elegance,
economy and adaptability, with the
concrete-framed buildings constructed to
shell and core stage on a fast-track
programme ready for customizing by
tenants. The façades incorporate extensive
sun screening as part of a low-energy
services agenda. Steel columns spaced
6–9 metres away from the blocks support
louvre screens, walkways and escape
stairs. The rigour of the concept and the
quality of the details set this scheme apart,
underlining the fact that quality architecture
can be achieved on a strict commercial
budget, a lesson that Lipton has been
preaching for two decades.

CITY HALL
LONDON BRIDGE CITY, SE1

FOSTER AND PARTNERS, 1998–2002

The new headquarters for the Mayor of London and the GLA was commissioned, controversially, well in advance of the elections held in 2000 that restored to London a measure of strategic local government. In 1998 competing proposals were put forward to house the GLA in Royal Victoria House, Bloomsbury, where a conversion by Will Alsop was on offer, and in a custom-made building developed as part of London Bridge City phase II. The latter option was selected by the government.

After a Classical Revival ('Venice on Thames') scheme designed by John Simpson was abandoned, a new masterplan for the second phase of London Bridge City was commissioned from Foster and Partners. The building can therefore be seen as a spin-off from a commercial development, located in an office ghetto removed from the 'real' London. Yet Foster's building, unkindly caricatured as a "glass testicle" or "fencing mask", is a carefully considered and highly symbolic structure that draws on his experience with the Berlin Reichstag. In total it provides 17,000 square metres of space on ten levels, with offices for mayor, GLA members and their staff, plus committee rooms and public space.

At the heart of the building, however, is the assembly chamber, enclosed in glass, with views across the Thames to the Tower of London. The symbolism is clear: this is a centre of transparent, democratic government, where the electors can watch their representatives at work. The public is welcome in this building (unlike the Palace of Westminster, where its presence is barely tolerated). A top-floor public space will be used for meetings, exhibitions and parties, and above that is a public rooftop terrace. The building is surrounded by a public piazza. Internal circulation via lifts and ramps provides access for all.

The form of the building has symbolic undertones but is also a reflection of a determined effort to secure optimum energy performance. Cladding has been designed to respond to patterns of sunlight falling on the building. Active and passive shading devices are part of a programme of natural ventilation, with cooling provided using ground water pumped from boreholes below the building, which looks set to become an instantly recognizable London landmark. Mayor Ken Livingstone was initially critical of the project, but the building could indirectly strengthen his campaign for extending local democracy in the capital.

J.C. DECAUX HEADQUARTERS
GREAT WEST ROAD, BRENTFORD
FOSTER AND PARTNERS, 1997–2000

Opposite, above
A new glazed 'street', used to display the company's products, separates the restored 1930s office wing from the new warehouse building designed by Foster and Partners for J.C. Decaux.

Opposite, below
The 1936 frontage to Great West Road has been immaculately restored as a setpiece of inter-war industrial architecture.

Below
The new warehouse is an innovative structure, designed for fast construction and flexible use.

Nikolaus Pevsner's famous dismissal of Wallis Gilbert's Hoover factory of 1932–38 – "perhaps the most offensive of the modernistic atrocities along this road of typical by-pass factories" – reflected a typically Modern Movement attitude to an architecture of show and, to Pevsner's mind, deceit. The Grade II listed former Curry factory, built in 1936, was another "by-pass factory" of the period, consisting of a flashy, symmetrical office building, broadly Deco in style, fronting the road, with a relatively utilitarian manufacturing shed hidden away behind. The typical

strategy in revamping buildings of this kind is to demolish the shed and replace it with another shed. At the Hoover factory itself, the famous office frontage is now the preface to a supermarket, with a smattering of Deco details to make the new development fit in.

Working for street furniture manufacturer J.C. Decaux, Foster was able to apply a more sophisticated approach. Foster has designed bus shelters, billboards and other items for the company, which has a serious commitment to good modern design. The office building has been restored in accord

with English Heritage requirements, a showpiece of 1930s architecture. The new warehouse behind is a highly innovative structure, built of pre-cast, thermally insulated concrete panels allowing fast-track construction. The interior is lit by a series of circular roof lights in the aluminium-clad roof, with the light fittings integrated into the assembly. The aim is to secure a warm and even glow inside the building in all conditions. Warehouse and offices are separated by a glazed 'street', which is used to display the company's products.

27–30 FINSBURY SQUARE, EC2

ERIC PARRY ARCHITECTS, 1999–2002

Eric Parry's redevelopment of nos. 27–30 Finsbury Square (on the edge of the City but just within the borough of Islington) highlights many of the issues underlying the politics of development in the business heart of London.

The site was previously occupied by two buildings, an undistinguished 1960s block deemed obsolete for present-day commercial use, and an inter-war building in a dignified, if commonplace, Classical manner, which was 'locally listed'. Both stood within a conservation area. Finsbury Square, a Georgian development in origin, is now a collection of diverse post-1900 frontages unified only by the prevalence of solid masonry façades: even Foster and Partners' recent building on the corner of Finsbury Pavement bows to this pattern.

Parry's project to redevelop the site was linked to a masterplan (by Latz & Partners) for the reconfiguration of the square,

a rather confused space that contains a bowling green, filling station and underground car park. The aim was to make the new building "a wall to a square", a distinctly civic presence. The sophisticated façade to the square, which is of loadbearing stone, engineered with Whitby & Bird, incorporates shading and drainage, and is integrated with the column-free office floors behind.

This is a subtly understated building by an architect whose thoughtful approach is increasingly influencing the London commercial scene. Parry sees the danger of a decreasing area for architecture in a market that demands standardization and economy. "Spaces need weight," he insists. At Finsbury Square he has produced a convincing model for a new masonry-fronted City architecture that is compatible with the spatial demands of the twenty-first-century office.

Right and opposite
The façade could be seen as an optional, even a dispensable, feature of the modern office building, but at Finsbury Square Eric Parry has transformed it into a potent civic and public presence.

HABERDASHERS' HALL, HOSIER LANE, EC1

MICHAEL HOPKINS & PARTNERS, 1996–2002

Below
The hall is housed in a collegiate-style quadrangle behind Smithfield. The palette of materials – load-bearing brick with a lead roof – is typical of Hopkins.

Opposite
Hopkins's reinterpretation of a great hall, with its diagrid roof and timber panelling, has a lightness that depends on the use of modern structural technology.

To outsiders, the culture of City livery companies is a mystery. Are these institutions little more than élitist dining clubs, a variant of freemasonry irrelevant to modern business? The fact that the Haberdashers' Company (first given a royal charter in 1448) supports eight schools, with over 6000 pupils, suggests that there is a little more to it than that (although haberdashers do not figure prominently in the commercial life of modern London).

The first Haberdashers' Hall burned in the Great Fire of London (1666); the second was destroyed by bombs in the Second World War. In recent years the company, with over 800 members, was housed in an undistinguished 1950s building by the obscure A.S. Ash, which was sold for redevelopment in the mid-1990s when the Haberdashers acquired a site at West Smithfield for their new hall. The site has been redeveloped with a new office building (a serviceable Hopkins design) along Hosier Lane and sixty-five apartments plus shops developed by British Land in a converted Edwardian block. The hall itself is housed in a central quadrangle at the secluded heart of the site.

The Haberdashers might seem a tailor-made Hopkins client. In recent years the Hopkins office has been adept at designing for old British institutions – public schools and colleges; Lord's Cricket Ground, in London; Goodwood racecourse, West Sussex; Glyndebourne opera house, East Sussex; even the House of Commons, in London. This is the world inhabited by City liverymen. As before, Hopkins has responded with a modern architecture rooted in history and finding expression in traditional materials; you would not expect a City company to commission Zaha Hadid or David Adjaye.

The starting-point of the project is the skiful strategy for the development of the site. In most circumstances, the plot would be the hardest to develop, surrounded as it is with previous developments, but it is the ideal location for the two-storey collegiate-style hall, entered via an arch off West Smithfield. The formal rooms – main dining-hall and other social spaces, court and committee rooms, and library – are on the first floor. Below are offices, cloakrooms, kitchens and other ancillary spaces arranged around a cloistered green quadrangle; on the north side the open cloister arcade is glazed in to form an orangery. There is a clear processional route from point of entry to dining-table.

The overall look of the building recalls Glyndebourne (and, for that matter, the residential block that Hopkins added to the Charterhouse, on the far side of Smithfield): loadbearing brick walls, finely detailed precast concrete left exposed, lead-covered roofs and high-quality timberwork. The approach embodies "a balance between change and tradition", say the architects. The livery hall is clearly the climax of the building. Its diagrid timber roof and oak panelling produce a rich and intimate atmosphere, modern but acceptable to the most entrenched traditionalist. This is well-crafted architecture with integrity and appropriateness, although it revisits familiar themes in the practice's work of the 1990s. The future direction of Hopkins's architecture is a matter of considerable interest.

HOME OFFICE AND HM PRISON SERVICE HEADQUARTERS, MARSHAM STREET, SW1

TERRY FARRELL & PARTNERS, 1991–2005

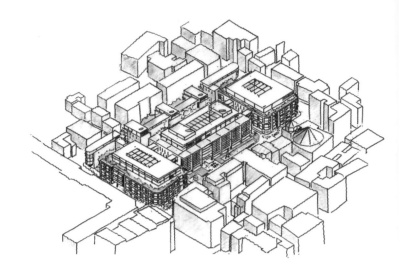

Terry Farrell's involvement with the site in Marsham Street that is now occupied by the Home Office extends back to 1991. The site was occupied for nearly thirty years by the three much-reviled high-rise office slabs designed by Eric Bedford for occupation by the Department of the Environment. In distant views along the Thames, the development, which was set on a high podium, provided a banal backdrop to the Palace of Westminster and Westminster Abbey. A decision to demolish it was finally taken in 1997 and the then Department of the Environment subsequently moved to new premises close to Victoria Station.

When Farrell prepared his 1991 masterplan for the redevelopment of the site, the relocation of the offices there was already under discussion and it was assumed that the site would be commercially redeveloped. The key principle of the masterplan was that

of permeability, and it is very much evident in the completed scheme: a series of distinct blocks, separated by public spaces and incorporating a mix of subsidiary uses, replaces the 1960s megastructure. The aim was to reintegrate the site into the historic city quarter around it. It was estimated that 50% more people than had worked in the wasteful 1960s slabs could be accommodated in new blocks no more than eight storeys high.

Farrell's involvement with Marsham Street continued through the 1990s, though in 1996, after a competition, a Classical Revival scheme by Italian architect Gabriele Taglieventi was selected for the site (and later quietly abandoned). Farrell's Home Office scheme, developed from 1998 onwards, provides space for 3000 staff. In line with government policy, the project was progressed on the basis of a Private Finance Initiative funding package. The

completed scheme consists of three linked buildings, a central block and two 'bookend' pavilions that extend to the junctions of Great Peter Street (to the north) and Horseferry Road (to the south). The central block has a distinctively civic look, with a great glazed screen fronting a grand internal entrance and reception space. The blocks are punctuated by 'pocket parks' and lit by glazed atria that guarantee pleasant, naturally lit workspaces for the civil servants. The materials mix, use of strong colour and incorporation of artworks gives a distinctive character to what are, in essence, high quality but extremely cost-effective office buildings. The project is a positive contribution to the process of repairing the urban fabric damaged by the excesses of dogmatic Modern Movement urban theories.

Left, above and opposite
Farrell's masterplan for Marsham Street replaces 1960s office slabs with a dense new urban quarter in which social and public spaces punctuate large office floorplates.

LLOYD'S REGISTER OF SHIPPING
FENCHURCH STREET, EC3
RICHARD ROGERS PARTNERSHIP, 1995–2000

Back in 1993 Richard Rogers had been commissioned to prepare a scheme to move Lloyd's Register, a venerable City institution, from Fenchurch Street to a green-belt site at Liphook, Hampshire. The organization saw little prospect of redeveloping in the conservation area around its splendid 1900s headquarters, but the proposed move to Hampshire foundered on planning objections. By 1995 Lloyd's Register had resolved to remain in the City and Rogers prepared a scheme that combined new construction with refurbishment. On Lloyd's Avenue, all existing façades had to be retained and the listed headquarters building was to be meticulously restored.

The site could not have been more problematic, with listed buildings and the remains of an ancient churchyard to cope with. Its confined nature made it difficult to ensure adequate amounts of natural light, though there were advantages in developing the new building within a protective shell of retained structures. An oasis of tranquil space, a quiet and relatively unpolluted refuge from the City streets, could be created, with the new building extending skywards within it to secure daylight and views.

As completed (and occupied since 2000), Lloyd's Register consists of two glazed slabs of accommodation, twelve and fourteen storeys tall, connected to six storeys of additional space behind retained façades on Lloyd's Avenue. The three buildings, arranged on a fan-shaped grid (which produced slightly tapered floorplates), are connected by glazed atriums. The former churchyard, long buried and forgotten within the City block, has re-emerged as an attractive public space, with the landscape extending into the internal atriums. The contrast between this ancient space and the transparent service towers, with fully glazed wall-climber lifts constantly in motion, reflects the dynamism of the twenty-first-century City. This is a finely crafted building, assembled of pre-cast concrete, with carefully detailed 'servant' cores for circulation and services made of brightly coloured steel.

The concrete structure of the building, left exposed in the office ceilings, with their chilled beams, is part of a strategy for low-energy running that also includes the use of extensive shading devices that give the east and west façades a strongly modelled character.

The balance of new design and conservation in this project is a response to the particular circumstances of the City; nobody doubted the importance of the original headquarters, for example. But the omission of Rogers's entrance pavilion on Fenchurch Street, an elegant structure, modestly slotted between Collcutt's 1901 building and a handsome listed pub, in favour of the retention of an unlisted building of no special interest was an example of the balance being lost.

Opposite
Rogers's Lloyd's Register develops the language of 'served and servant' spaces seen in his earlier City masterpiece, Lloyd's of London, using a high degree of glazing to channel natural light into the confined site.

Above
Lofty glazed atriums separate the office wings and filter controlled daylight into workspaces.

LONDON BRIDGE TOWER, SE1

RENZO PIANO BUILDING WORKSHOP/BROADWAY MALYAN, 2000–05

The London Bridge Tower could become, like Norman Foster's Millennium Tower, one of London's great unbuilts. Firmly opposed by English Heritage and other interests, it could remain as nothing more than a vision. Yet one has to take developer Irvine Sellar seriously when he speaks of a "global landmark ... a building of which Londoners can be rightly proud": projects such as this are not the most obvious way to make profits out of property and, like all tower-builders, Sellar seems to be driven by considerations wider than the purely financial.

Initial proposals were drawn up by Broadway Malyan, but towards the end of 2000 the Genoese master Renzo Piano was brought in to rethink the scheme, intended to replace a dreary 1970s office tower adjacent to London Bridge station. At this stage, the new building was to be 390 metres high, easily the tallest habitable building in Europe. By the time of the planning submission in 2001, its height had been cut to 306 metres – not enough of a reduction to satisfy the anti-tower lobby. London mayor Ken Livingstone, however, emerged as a strong supporter of the project, which also won backing from the Commission for Architecture and the Built Environment. With 80,000 square metres of office, hotel and residential space over a main transport hub, the tower is in accord with Livingstone's environmental and regenerative strategies and would be a huge booster to the economy of Southwark.

Piano has compared his designs to "a shard of glass" – he considers the slender, spire-like form of the tower a positive addition to the London skyline and believes that its presence will be far more ethereal than opponents of the scheme allege. Piano's preoccupation with the appropriate use of materials – stone, wood, steel, glass – is famous and has produced a diverse range of buildings. At London Bridge, he proposes a sophisticated use of glazing, with expressive façades of angled panes intended to reflect light and the changing patterns of the sky, so that the perceived form of the building will vary with the weather and the seasons. It will be anchored to the site by a base containing shops, restaurants and exhibition and conference spaces where up to ten thousand people could work.

Oddly, the projections of the tower's impact used as ammunition by its opponents do not make it look overbearing. Rather, it appears as a memorable landmark, far removed from the conventional idea of an office block. It may well be unbuildable, but if it were to be built it would become an instant symbol of London.

Below and opposite
Renzo Piano's London Bridge Tower has been designed as a light and transparent needle, a shapely contrast to the lumpish slabs that surround the site, and sits comfortably in the historic Borough district.

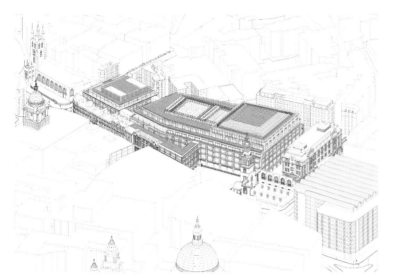

MERRILL LYNCH FINANCIAL CENTRE
NEWGATE, EC1

SWANKE HAYDEN CONNELL ARCHITECTS, 1996–2001

The Merrill Lynch development at Newgate, close to St Paul's Cathedral, is – at 80,000 square metres – one of London's largest office schemes. It is remarkable, however, not only for its scale, but also for its positive impact on the public realm and imaginative approach to the reuse of historic buildings. Swanke Hayden Connell Architects (SHCA), like Merrill Lynch a firm with American roots, was brought in soon after a business merger, gathering various arms of the company under one roof, made the construction of new premises a priority. None of the buildings on offer, either completed or planned, was suitable for Merrill Lynch's requirements, which included space for very large dealing floors. The company therefore acquired the site at Newgate, largely occupied by a redundant postal sorting office, which until the 1900s had been the site of the public school Christ's Hospital and, before the Reformation in the sixteenth century, of the London house of the Franciscan order. On the eastern edge of the site stands the remains of Sir Christopher Wren's Christ Church, gutted by wartime bombs and partly demolished as late as the 1970s for road widening – an appalling act of vandalism. The southern edge of the site is enclosed by a run of Victorian buildings, which the City had long planned to raze for yet more road surface but had effectively conceded would have to be retained and refurbished.

Under the Merrill Lynch scheme the former sorting office, a listed building, was demolished with the approval of English Heritage, which agreed that it had no potential for reuse. A very large block housing two trading floors, each of more than 6000 square metres, now occupies the centre of the site. Another new block addresses Giltspur Street to the west. To the east, the former post office has been refurbished as a conference and exhibition space. The architecture of the new buildings is dignified, solid and unfussy, with brick and stone cladding framing large window openings, an approach that contrasts with the blatant façadism of much Post-modernist work of the 1980s. An impressive glazed galleria connects the dealing-floor block with retained buildings on Newgate Street.

The chief success of the scheme, however, lies in its expansion and improvement of the public routes and spaces within the site. A generous cloister frames the former churchyard of Christ Church, which has been landscaped as an attractive garden, with its lost railings reinstated. A further public route extends from Newgate Street behind the restored Victorian buildings; the ground floors are let as shops and cafés. The scheme shows how large modern financial operations can be accommodated, quite painlessly, at the heart of the City. The pity is that there is probably no other comparable site available in the Square Mile – hence the ongoing push into Spitalfields and Shoreditch.

Left and opposite
Highly contextual externally, the Merrill Lynch development includes a covered internal street that is part of a replanning of the entire site to provide new public routes.

THE MINERVA BUILDING, ALDGATE, EC3
NICHOLAS GRIMSHAW & PARTNERS, 1999–

Grimshaw's Minerva tower (designed for client Minerva plc) is one of the most promising of the various proposals for tall buildings in and around the City of London that emerged in the first years of the twenty-first century. The present (2002) scheme is Grimshaw's second for the Aldgate site; its predecessor, commissioned in 1999, a tower of rather squat proportions notable for the scale of the floorplates it offered, was abandoned after receiving a cool reception from City planners and the Commission for Architecture and the Built Environment (CABE). It is interesting to note that Minerva's existing planning consent, granted in 1999, provided for a fourteen-storey block with 46,500 square metres of office space, whereas Grimshaw's building will be 217 metres tall with 93,000 square metres of lettable space – the largest free-standing office building in the City.

The City-fringe site, at the junction of Houndsditch and St Botolph Street, was historically a gateway to the Square Mile, a fact that underlines the case for a landmark structure there. The 1980s office boom extended to Aldgate: one of the most prominent neighbours is the direly Post-modernist Beaufort House of 1986–88. Objections to the Minerva tower have focused both on its impact on the City skyline and on its relationship to the Georgian church of St Botolph, yet this could be an exciting juxtaposition, just as I.M. Pei's crystalline Hancock Tower provides a striking backdrop to Trinity Church in Boston, Massachusetts. At present, the church is marooned on a traffic island, so the Minerva scheme could be the catalyst for a radical reconfiguration of the surrounding area. Existing buildings to be demolished include an ugly multi-storey car park.

The elegant (but quite complex) form of the building reflects its operational agenda: it could be a wholly occupied headquarters or easily be subdivided, in line with the demands of the market. The architects see it as a series of open books of varying height, the asymmetry of the plan, with four façade planes dividing the site diagonally, responding to the context of streets and routes. The theme of asymmetry extends into the section of the building. The repetitive floor pattern of the past is jettisoned in favour of a sophisticated mix of spaces. The sky lobby, halfway up the tower, is the social heart of the building, accessed directly by double-decker express lifts. The ground floor contains 2000 square metres of retailing served by new pedestrian arcades. The rooftop restaurant has its own dedicated lift service.

Grimshaw's concern for detail is famous and there is no doubt that this will be a finely crafted building. As is now customary, the developer argues that it would also be 'sustainable', a claim always hard to quantify. Double-skin façades, with opening windows on the inner skin, and an element of natural ventilation – although conventional air-conditioning is also provided – could, however, significantly reduce energy usage.

Above and opposite
The Minerva Building is conceived as a series of intersecting planes breaking down the mass of the structure and responding to its urban context. The building would be an elegant addition to the eastern quarter of the City.

Left and opposite, bottom
The redevelopment of Paddington Basin regenerates a forgotten area in the hinterland of Paddington Station.

Opposite, top
Terry Farrell's The Point was the first building on the site to be completed: its wedge shape responds to the curve in the Grand Union Canal at this point.

PADDINGTON BASIN, W2
TERRY FARRELL & PARTNERS/
RICHARD ROGERS PARTNERSHIP, 2000–

The area around Paddington station – a ten-acre site focusing on the basin of the Grand Union Canal, plus the former Great Western Railway goods yard – forms the largest development site in the City of Westminster, potentially a Canary Wharf for central London. The model of Canary Wharf, indeed – lots of offices plus housing for the affluent – seems to have fuelled the ongoing plans for the site, though the area might have been integrated into the city and become a model for mixed-use development.

Paddington has had a long wait for the regeneration bandwagon. A 110,000-square-metre office project for the Basin, plus retailing and residential development, designed by Building Design Partnership and Skidmore, Owings & Merrill, won detailed planning consent in 1992 but fell victim to the recession. Renewed developer interest in the area has been partly stimulated by transport improvements – the Heathrow Express, the prospect of CrossRail (first planned in the 1980s) actually happening, and the proposed reconstruction and extension of the mainline station, with new links to the goods yard and Basin. The goods yard is now being transformed by Development Securities, with an intensive 175,000-square-metre office and residential scheme masterplanned by Sidell Gibson (previous plans for the site were drawn up by Seifert & Partners).

The Basin development was successfully relaunched by a partnership between Godfrey Bradman of European Land and Property and Chelsfield's Elliott Bernerd. The masterplan was prepared by Terry Farrell and provides for a more dynamic mix, in terms of scale and forms, than was envisaged in the early 1990s. Phase one, on the north side of the Basin, will contain 140,000 square metres of offices and apartments.

The Point, designed by Farrell, was the first of the buildings to be completed. A ten-storey, 20,500-square-metre wedge-shaped office scheme with the sleek styling typical of Farrell's recent work, it forms a gateway to the Basin. Richard Rogers Partnership is responsible for two linked blocks on the canalside, though a mixed-use tower located on the northerly edge of the site, close to the A40, seems unlikely to be built.

The reconstruction of Paddington station by Network Rail will include a major office scheme designed by Nicholas Grimshaw. Plans for a forty-two-storey tower were announced in 2000, with a new public concourse to the canal. The tower, however, has been abandoned in Grimshaw's latest proposals for the station.

PALESTRA, BLACKFRIARS ROAD, SE1
ALSOP ARCHITECTS, 1999–

The Palestra project – a 28,000-square-metre landmark office building opposite Richard MacCormac's Southwark station – is a product of the 'Southwark effect', the boom in development south of the river fuelled by the Jubilee line extension and Tate Modern and facilitated by an enterprise-friendly local authority and the dynamic regeneration agenda set by planner Fred Manson. The scheme reflects Will Alsop's steady rise to the centre of the London scene and his clear emergence as a front-rank commercial architect: his designs are no longer seen as fanciful or unbuildable.

The building replaces Orbit House, an unremarkable 1960s block by Seifert that provided a depressing introduction to the borough for millions of Tate Modern visitors using Southwark station. Proximity to the Underground was a strong attraction, while the prospect of Thameslink 2000 operating from nearby Blackfriars, with regular airport links, contributes to its appeal.

The key idea of the scheme is that of a series of horizontal planes, the lowest tilted off the ground to provide a dynamic public space that recognizes the new role of Southwark as a tourist location, with streets full of people. The central office zone of the building forms a 'cloud' floating above Southwark. A proposed top slab, containing executive offices, was later deleted on the recommendation of planners. Palestra not only looks radical – its polychromatic façades make use of the latest glazing technology, with ceramic inks indelibly bonded into the glass, to break down the rigid geometry of the office floors – but equally represents a fresh look at the large office building. The 30-metre-wide floors are designed for maximum flexibility and are enhanced by double-height spaces, mezzanines and terraces. An intermediate glazed zone between the first and second planes provides a social space for the building's users, a recognition of the primacy of interaction in the new office. At street level, cafés and shops cater for both building users and for the public: the barrier between the office and the public domain is eroded.

Left, above and opposite
Will Alsop's Palestra is a landmark development in the transformation of the Bankside area – it replaces a banal 1960s block – and is innovative in form, in materials and in its radical view of the workplace, as well as its contribution to the public realm.

PATERNOSTER SQUARE
CITY OF LONDON, EC4

WHITFIELD PARTNERS (MASTERPLAN)/ALLIES & MORRISON/
MacCORMAC JAMIESON PRICHARD/SIDELL GIBSON/
ERIC PARRY ARCHITECTS/SHEPPARD ROBSON, 1997–2004

Included here as the distinctly downbeat conclusion to a long-running saga that has involved many of the biggest names in British architecture and a succession of owners/developers, the Paternoster Square development, yards from St Paul's Cathedral, occupies one of the most prominent sites in the whole of London. The location had the potential to generate a new quarter of outstanding quality: what has been built is safe and inoffensive rather than challenging.

The dense area of Victorian offices and warehouses around the old Paternoster Square was levelled by German bombs in 1940. It was rebuilt, in line with a masterplan by Sir William Holford and with Trehearne & Norman as architects, in 1961–67 as a rather bland complex of offices set on a raised service deck around public spaces which, though generous in scale, were always underused. Never much loved, the rebuilt seven-acre quarter seemed an obvious location for the deep-plan office spaces demanded by the post-'Big Bang' City. In 1986 a starry team of practices, including Foster, Rogers, Stirling, Skidmore, Owings & Merrill, Isozaki and MacCormac, was invited to prepare redevelopment proposals. The more radical ideas – such as Foster's 'souk' of interlocking office spaces and pedestrian routes and Rogers's dramatic daylit Underground concourse – found no favour and a classically inclined (though formally modern) scheme by Arup Associates was selected in 1987. Though subsequently beefed up with contributions from Michael Hopkins and Richard MacCormac, the Arup masterplan was later dropped after strident criticism from the Prince of Wales (whose influence was then at its zenith). The prince

backed alternative, Classical Revival plans by John Simpson, strongly influenced by the urban thinking of Leon Krier. After a change of developers, Simpson was brought in as masterplanner, working – uncomfortably, perhaps – with Terry Farrell (then in Post-modernist mode) and American Thomas Beeby. Individual blocks were designed by Demetri Porphyrios, Quinlan Terry and others. The scheme got planning consent in 1993 and was then quietly abandoned. Sir William Whitfield, a senior figure adept at marrying modernity and tradition and a former Surveyor of St Paul's, was brought in as masterplanner in 1997.

The redevelopment of Paternoster Square was completed with the unveiling of the resited Temple Bar (brought from a field in Hertfordshire) in 2004. Whitfield has given London a decent new square, though some details of the masterplan grate: the heavy sub-classical loggias, for example, and the rather whimsical column (incorporating ventilation ducts for underground service routes) which forms a rather lame 'feature'. Of the new buildings, that by Eric Parry is perhaps the most satisfactory, since Parry's rationalism seems in tune with the context. Allies & Morrison, Sheppard Robson and Sidell Gibson all play the game, producing architecture that is essentially background; but maybe this is what was needed on this site? Richard MacCormac's block on the west side of the square is, in contrast, perhaps too assertive, while Whitfield's replacement for Juxon House, at the top of Ludgate Hill, is something of an embarrassment, a weak exercise in stripped classicism of the sort that Victor Heal was doing to better effect in the City fifty years ago.

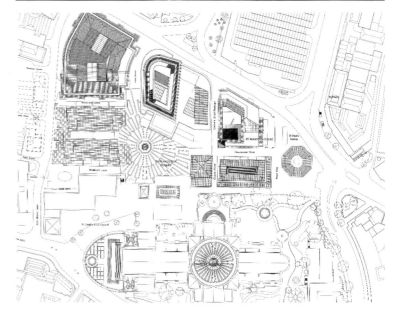

Right and opposite
To a masterplan by William Whitfield, the
redevelopment of Paternoster Square includes
buildings by a number of major architectural
practices in a contextual modern manner,
with buildings framing views of St Paul's Cathedral.
An irregular square forms the centrepiece of
the scheme. St Martin's Court (right and below),
by Allies & Morrison, focuses on an internal glazed
atrium that connects the square to Newgate Street.

PORTCULLIS HOUSE
(NEW PARLIAMENTARY BUILDING)
VICTORIA EMBANKMENT, SW1

MICHAEL HOPKINS & PARTNERS, 1989–2000

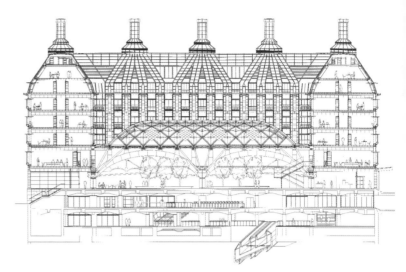

After several decades of indecision – an earlier project for an extension to the Houses of Parliament by Spence & Webster was abandoned – the commission for a new parliamentary building, with office and committee room accommodation for the House of Commons, went to Michael Hopkins & Partners in 1989. In the same year, legislation providing for the construction of the Jubilee line extension, with a new interchange station at Westminster, was tabled. With the existing Underground station located directly underneath the site of what became Portcullis House, the two projects seemed inseparable. In 1991 Hopkins was appointed architect for the new station and construction began early in 1994. After Members of Parliament vetoed the idea of a station concourse below Parliament Square, the new booking hall was to be sited directly beneath the central courtyard of the new parliamentary building, with the District line tracks operating throughout construction work a level below. The structure of Portcullis House is integrated with that of the station, and the two projects, both completed during 2000, ran in parallel. The great columns on which Portcullis House stands extend down 40 metres into the station box, accommodating the diagonal route of the District line and the banks of escalators serving the Jubilee line platforms.

The structural challenge of the project was enormous. Given the cultural and architectural climate of 1980s Britain, however, the aesthetic challenge of designing a contemporary building adjacent to Pugin and Barry's Palace of Westminster, a national icon, was hardly less daunting. The completed building takes its scale from Norman Shaw's neighbouring Scotland Yard (now used by the Commons), which also provides the cue for the massive thermal chimneys. The picturesque if rather industrial chimneys are integral to a low-energy ventilation strategy, also reflected in a plan that disposes naturally lit offices around a central court. At ground-floor level the court forms a social and circulation space for the complex, enclosed by a finely crafted roof of glass, laminated timber and steel – a reinterpretation of the innovative tradition which inspired the great fourteenth-century roof of Westminster Hall, which sits on the six main structural columns. Largely inaccessible to the public, this is one of the most impressive contemporary spaces in London, connected by tunnel to the Palace of Westminster. The exterior of Portcullis House below roof level is more mannered, though its logic is impeccable: vertical stone bands, diminishing in width as they rise, frame window bays formed of bronze. Planned under Thatcher and opened under Blair, Portcullis House is genuinely contextual – and more innovative than some negative critics allow. Built to last a century, it has already become an accepted part of the riverside scene. Will it outlive the institution it houses?

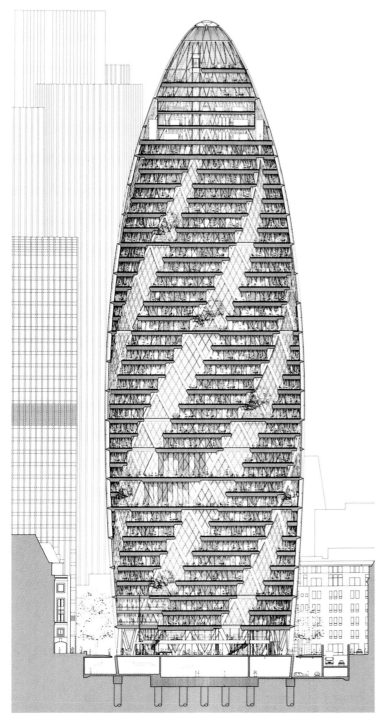

SWISS RE HEADQUARTERS
30 ST MARY AXE, EC3
FOSTER AND PARTNERS, 1997–2004

Swiss Re was one of half a dozen or more City of London office schemes by Foster and Partners on site or planned in 2001. It stands out from the rest in terms not only of its prominence on the skyline – at forty-one storeys, it competes for attention with the slightly taller Tower 42 (formerly NatWest Tower) – but even more for its technical and environmental innovation. Indeed, Swiss Re is one of the key Foster projects of the new century, and was a worthy recipient of the coveted Stirling Prize in 2004.

The site is that of the Baltic Exchange, a sumptuous but rather dim Edwardian commercial palazzo damaged beyond repair by an IRA bomb in 1992. Foster's first proposal for the site was the London Millennium Tower, a proposal that aroused strong opposition from amenity groups and found little favour with the City Corporation. With Swiss Re (a major reinsurance company) as client, Foster developed a new scheme for "London's first ecological tall building". The 40,000-square-metre project has its origins in Norman Foster's exploratory work with Buckminster Fuller on the Climatroffice, where green garden spaces would be integrated into the workplace, and develops ideas seen in the seminal 1970s Willis Faber offices and, more recently, in the Frankfurt

Left
The Swiss Re tower is innovative both structurally and environmentally: a series of internal gardens is a key element of the building.

Opposite
The building has a distinctive and dramatic presence on the skyline, its shapely form contrasting with the more conventional geometry of earlier buildings in the City.

Commerzbank (with its 'sky gardens'). Foster's partner Ken Shuttleworth has compared Swiss Re to "a series of Willis Fabers, piled vertically, one on top of the other". A developed version of the Commerzbank sky garden is used both as a social focus and as part of a low-energy environmental strategy: stale air will be drawn into the gardens and re-oxygenated by the dense planting. (Ventilation is largely by natural, non-mechanical means; air conditioning is used only in a supplementary role and windows are made to open.) The office floors spiral around the gardens, forming vertical 'villages' that are intended to generate the interaction increasingly seen as vital to creative office work. Lifts, stairs and other services are concentrated in a central core, leaving the fully glazed perimeter free of intrusions.

At street level the painstaking aerodynamic modelling of the tower has been calculated to avoid down draughts and ensure benign conditions in the new piazza that surrounds the building. Two floors of the building will be given over to a shopping arcade.

Swiss Re has injected a new element into a continuing debate about the place of high buildings in London. It reinforces the point that office towers can be distinctive, even beautiful, objects that complement, rather than deface, the skyline. It also undermines the contention that tall buildings are environmentally irresponsible, dependent on huge amounts of energy. For all this, it is a prestige commission, a bespoke work for a client whose name and reputation can only benefit from an act of enlightened patronage.

TALKBACK HEADQUARTERS NEWMAN STREET, W1

BUSCHOW HENLEY, 1999–2001

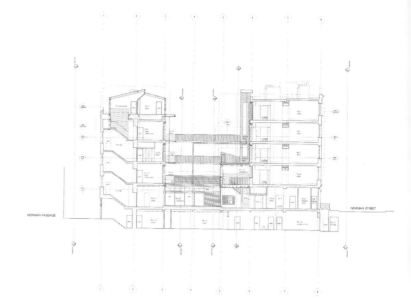

Buschow Henley's mixed-use adaptation at Shepherdess Walk, Hoxton, was an object lesson in how to reuse old industrial buildings, adding new elements without draining them of character and patina. The youthful practice's strong concern for materials and their appropriate use was reflected in the project. The new headquarters for TalkBack TV just north of Oxford Street embraces similar concerns, though both location and the raw material that forms the basis of the project are very different.

TalkBack TV is a production company with a strong creative bent that employs up to two hundred and fifty people. The commissioning of its new London base involved the development not only of a functional brief but also a searching examination of the ethos and aspirations of the company, which sees itself as straddling the worlds of business and research/education. It is concerned with ideas and with individuals, a non-hierarchical organization that is about interaction and communication. In the past, it has inhabited a string of premises across the West End. The informality of this arrangement, but not its inconvenience, is valued.

The new building is an adaptation of two six-storey blocks, sturdily built but of uncertain date (c.1900) and no special architectural interest, on Newman Street,

separated by a courtyard from a rear five-storey block on to the narrow Newman Passage. The architects' proposal was to form a multi-storey cloister by demolishing a two-storey linking block and inserting a new structure into the gap. This structure houses communal facilities for the complex, with a reception area and meeting and common rooms around an open court. Studio spaces are at basement level, insulated from noise. First-floor roof gardens are part of an effort to create a quiet oasis, apparently removed from the noisy streets beyond. The central space is the focus of the development, with offices served by timber decks that are intended as places of interaction as well as of circulation. The Newman Passage building has been given an additional floor. Timber is used extensively, along with galvanized steel, zinc and aluminium; existing brickwork, in generally good condition, has been left much as found. The lift tower has been made into a landmark 'campanile', clad in Douglas fir boarding, with a cut-away at the top to expose the works.

This project illustrates the way in which relatively ordinary buildings can be given a unique quality and customized to the needs of state-of-the-art organizations. Buschow Henley's project transforms what existed, but equally responds to the secret world of backyards and rooftops behind the blank Victorian façades.

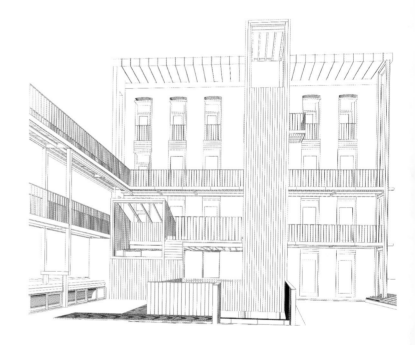

Above
The TalkBack project colonizes a previously underused area at the core of a West End block, linking two existing buildings with a new block containing the reception area and meeting rooms.

Opposite
The additions to the Victorian blocks have been made in a lightweight manner, using a variety of materials, including the Douglas fir cladding applied to the new lift shaft.

WELLCOME TRUST HEADQUARTERS
EUSTON ROAD, NW1

HOPKINS ARCHITECTS, 1999–2004

Below
The view from Euston Road (top) and
from Gower Place at the back (bottom).

Opposite
The glazed atrium forms the social hub of the
building, with office floors open to the central
space, and a top-floor restaurant.

Commissioned by a charitable foundation that funds more than a fifth of medical research worldwide, Hopkins's Wellcome Trust building stands adjacent to the trust's former headquarters on Euston Road, a 1930s classical palazzo now being converted by Hopkins into a conference, exhibition and education centre freely open to the public. For all its striking transparency, the new headquarters is in essence a bespoke office building occupied by more than five hundred staff.

A new component in the academic and medical quarter of Bloomsbury – University College London's main campus adjoins to the south and the new PFI-funded tower of University College Hospital lies just across Gower Street – the Gibbs Building (as it is formally known) squares up to the noisy Euston Road with ten storeys of fully glazed office floors, its bulk broken down by vertical service towers and 'mini atria' (intended as break-out points for meetings and for the informal encounters that are seen as vital to creative working). To the south, on Gower Place (now repaved, traffic-calmed and landscaped), it falls away to five storeys, capped by a staff restaurant. A sweeping roof, part metallic and part glazed, encloses parallel office wings joined by a full-height atrium, one of the most spectacular seen in London for some time. This is a building in which architecture and structure are indivisible: sophisticated fire engineering allows the steel frame to be fully exposed internally, though its austerity is softened by the use of timber veneers and extensive planting. A spectacular artwork by Thomas Heatherwick, entirely in

tune with its setting, is located at the western end of the atrium, foiling views out to the ungainly University College Hospital tower. The ground floor of the building, though not open to the public, is essentially social space, with meeting and conference rooms (the trust is a focus for the British medical and scientific community) and a café. One by-product of the project has been a substantial improvement to passenger facilities at Euston Square Underground station, the main concourse of which lies below the building; a new glazed and naturally lit staircase hall now provides access to the station.

This building makes no pretence of being anything but what it is: a corporate headquarters, though one with a function (the distribution rather than accumulation of money) rather different to others of its kind. It is the generosity of the project, in terms not only of space but also of quality of detail and fit-out, that sets it apart. A meeting place as well as a workplace, the new headquarters balances comfort with an element of dynamism that should inspire users. Given that all this was achieved to a budget more typical of superior speculative office buildings than costly corporate gestures – the client was anxious to combine quality with appropriate economy – the project is an exemplar for new workplace design. It is also a marker for the ongoing redevelopment of the Euston Road/Marylebone Road, which has the potential to become an enjoyable urban boulevard rather than the noisy and polluted urban freeway that it has been for too long.

WINCHESTER HOUSE, LONDON WALL, EC2

SWANKE HAYDEN CONNELL, 1995–99

The shifting tide of planning and design policies in the City – ranging from determinedly preservationist to ardently *laissez-faire* – poses enormous problems for developers seeking to provide for global financial industries. By 2001 the City was looking favourably on proposals for tall buildings and questioning established conservation strategies. A few years earlier, the discreet ground-scraper was *de rigueur*. Swanke Hayden Connell's Winchester House remains one of the best examples of the genre. (The same practice has more recently completed an even larger building for Merrill Lynch, buried behind retained frontages at Newgate.)

Pevsner described the 1960s Winchester House, demolished for this development, as "reticent and anonymous" – dull and mean would be equally suitable adjectives for this twenty-two-storey tower, which occupied only 25% of the total site area. The redevelopment had to take account (as the 1960s scheme did not) of the group of listed buildings, including the Neo-classical church of All Hallows, that surround the site. The existence of a vast parking basement was a 1960s asset worth retaining: it was used for plant and services, rather than parking, to free the upper levels of the new building.

The new Winchester House fills the site, reinstating the dignity of the narrow Great Winchester Street (previously downgraded to a service road). On this elevation the scheme is broken down into a series of units – town houses – in deference to the scale of the street. On London Wall the use of set-backs reduces the apparent bulk and height of the ten-storey building. Sandstone is used to good effect as a cladding material; during the late 1990s, stone facings were inevitably imposed on all City developments. The leasing of the building to Deutsche Bank, famous as a patron of contemporary art, has made the exceptionally generous reception area into a gallery. How unfortunate that the public can only peer through the glass doors.

Left
The unusually generous reception lobby is used as a gallery for the display of an outstanding collection of contemporary art.

Right and opposite
The use of stone cladding and set-backs gives the London Wall elevation a scale and dignity appropriate to its context and represents a bold reversal of the tower/piazza planning of the 1960s, while the rear elevation is articulated to address a minor City street.

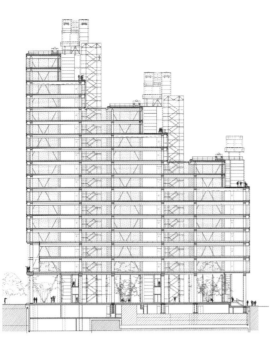

88 WOOD STREET, EC2
RICHARD ROGERS PARTNERSHIP, 1990–99

88 Wood Street was Richard Rogers's first City building since the completion of Lloyd's of London in 1986. The commission came to the practice in 1990, when the brief was for a prestige headquarters for the Japanese Daiwa corporation. Delays in securing consent to demolish a listed building on the site proved fatal to this project: recession in London and the Far East killed it.

When Daiwa revived the scheme in 1993, it was with the intention of building a straightforward speculative office development. The existing proposals could not be adapted to the changed brief and the project was entirely redesigned in 1993–94 and constructed in 1995–99.

The completed building consists of three linked parallel blocks that step up from eight storeys on Wood Street (where the development faces the Grade I-listed Wren tower of St Alban's church and the Neo-classical police station by McMorran & Whitby) to fourteen and finally to eighteen storeys.

88 Wood Street has the strong stamp of the Rogers office. The tower-like service cores, for example, are in the Lloyd's tradition, but plant was banished, as far as possible, to the basement so that the slender towers of the three primary cores contain only toilets and lifts, with highly glazed staircases attached. The lifts sit within a glazed enclosure, so that transparency is combined with protection from the weather. The service towers are steel-framed, while the main structure is of concrete, though the steel bracing reinforces the metallic look of the building. Colour is used boldly, in the Rogers manner, on the staircases and sculptural services extractors at street level.

The context of the scheme is mostly post-war and extraordinarily varied: the Rogers building is sandwiched between unremarkable new office developments by Foster and Partners and Sheppard Robson and slammed up against Terry Farrell's showy 1980s Albangate, with the dramatic towers of the Barbican as a backcloth. It stands out in this setting as something more than a 'good ordinary' City office building. It is the transparency and lightness of 88 Wood Street that is memorable, achieved firstly by skilful massing that allows natural light to permeate the office floors. The use of crystal-clear glass, with floor-to-ceiling panels within the grid, is uncompromising in a way that is typical of Rogers. The entrance lobby has a nobility of scale rarely found in Britain, with internal and external landscape merging to embrace the remains of an ancient churchyard. London needs more commercial architecture of this quality.

Opposite
The entrance lobby at 88 Wood Street is one of the grandest in London, its luminous interior seamlessly linked to the reconfigured external landscape.

Above
The building consists of three linked blocks, the lowest facing Wood Street, with services used in typical Rogers fashion to articulate the architecture.

SHOPS

CARTIER, OLD BOND STREET
JEAN-MICHEL WILMOTTE

MARNI, SLOANE STREET
FUTURE SYSTEMS

PETER JONES, SLOANE SQUARE
JOHN McASLAN + PARTNERS

SAINSBURY'S, GREENWICH PENINSULA
CHETWOOD ASSOCIATES

CARTIER, 40–41 OLD BOND STREET, W1
JEAN-MICHEL WILMOTTE, 2000

While many fashion retailers aim at spectacular and even bizarre effects in their premises, Cartier has sought a more classic, though essentially contemporary, elegance, combining tradition with modernity, in its series of boutiques designed by French architect Jean-Michel Wilmotte. The first two opened in Paris and Tokyo in 1999.

The façade of the new London shop is made from slate, a matt material that effectively frames the anti-reflection glass of the windows and provides the element of sobriety, tranquility and restraint that the client desired. Sparkling black Norwegian stone is used for the internal façade, while the floors are laid in pale Italian stone. The woodwork is a mixture of grained oak and rosewood, with metallic finishes of velvet nickel. Wilmotte's fit-out draws on his extensive experience of public and museum commissions – for example, the interiors of the Grand Louvre. Furniture was specially designed by Pierre Deltombe (whose previous jobs include the design of the visitor facilities at the Sainte-Chapelle in Paris) while diffused lighting animates the 'jewel box' interior with its series of intimate spaces.

In Britain, 'luxury' usually implies a firmly traditional look that often descends to weak pastiche: London lacks classic modern retail interiors. (Simpson's, Piccadilly, was spoiled by conversion to a bookstore.) Wilmotte's work for Cartier has a timeless quality that combines elegance and a suggestion of minimalism with the degree of comfort and reassurance that anyone considering spending £50,000 on an engagement ring might appreciate.

Left and opposite
Cartier's new London shop makes use of high-quality materials – stone, wood, leather and glass – to achieve an effect that is opulent without being showy, in keeping with the company's image.

MARNI, SLOANE STREET, SW3
FUTURE SYSTEMS, 2000

Shops come and go: twenty-five years ago, Norman Foster's wonderfully light and elegant store for Joseph was one of the sights of Sloane Street. Jan Kaplicky and Amanda Levete of Future Systems come out of Foster's high-tech stable, but their work has a sensual, illusionistic, even baroque, quality that Foster eschews. They are, in other words, natural shop designers and the Marni store is in a tradition of retail design that includes major works in London by David Chipperfield, Branson Coates and others. Selfridge's commission to the practice to design a new store in Birmingham was an extraordinary breakthrough.

The shop makes its mark on the style-conscious street with a frontage forged of stainless steel membrane, a mere 1.3 millimetres thick. Inside, the space is typically long and narrow. The clothes are hung or displayed on rails formed as steel trees cantilevered out of the floor: the merchandise is as much the focus of the place as the art in a gallery.

The backcloth to the interior is strongly coloured, forming a contrast to the stark white flooring, formed of reconstituted glass and seen as floating independent of its setting. Furniture is kept to a bare minimum: the cash desk is formed within one of the steel rail structures. At one time, high fashion courted architectural minimalism, seeing it as a good background for displaying the goods. Future Systems' work demands attention and is anything but minimal. Architecture and fashion merge to form a magic world – alas, one that may prove all too ephemeral.

Right and opposite
Future Systems' Marni store is extraordinary for its use of vivid colour and unusual materials (the floor is of reconstituted glass) and for its rejection of the customary shop fittings in favour of a system of steel rails and trees.

PETER JONES, SLOANE SQUARE, SW3

JOHN McASLAN + PARTNERS, 1997–2004

The Peter Jones store is one of the few modern buildings in London that has been almost universally popular since the first phase of William Crabtree's scheme, with its great curving curtain wall on to Sloane Square, was constructed in 1935–37. Crabtree was rebuilding an existing department store. The Second World War brought work to a standstill, and elements of the Victorian building were retained when the project was eventually completed in the 1960s to a compromised version of the original scheme. Inside, some awkward spaces were created, with poor connections between departments, though the progressive outlook of the John Lewis

Partnership ensured that staff facilities, which included a theatre and squash courts, were a priority.

John McAslan's phased £100,000,000 reconstruction aimed to address the failings of the existing building and finally to realize the promise of Crabtree's extraordinary vision. Floor levels were rationalized, the disjunctions within the building addressed, and new servicing and storage areas created. At the heart of the store, a spectacular new central light well rises seven storeys to the roof, with escalators serving all floors. Services have been entirely renewed, with a progressive energy strategy that makes use of chilled beams –

for the first time in a British retail development – to cool the spaces. Existing façades have been seamlessly upgraded in line with modern environmental standards.

Externally Peter Jones remains the modern landmark it has always been, but it has been re-equipped to retain its position as one of London's best-loved shops. This project set a new benchmark for the sympathetic rehabilitation of classic Modern Movement buildings, all carried out with the store open to customers and within the context of a site tightly surrounded by busy streets.

Left
The exterior of Peter Jones, a 1930s Modern Movement classic.

Above and opposite
The interior reconstruction provides a new full-height atrium with escalators serving all floors, and addresses the shortcomings of an awkwardly planned interior completed, to a compromised plan, in the 1960s.

SAINSBURY'S, GREENWICH PENINSULA, SE10
CHETWOOD ASSOCIATES, 1996–2000

Back in the late 1980s, Sainsbury's surprised the world of food retailing by commissioning Nicholas Grimshaw to design its new branch in Camden Town. It was a bold move, though the interior of the store is a standard Sainsbury's fit-out of the period – as if the client's nerve had failed well into the project. Nonetheless, the development, including ten town houses and some workshops, provided a refreshing contrast to the sub-vernacular style favoured by other chains.

The store at the Greenwich Peninsula was bound to be seen as something of a demonstration project, given the high aspirations of the masterplan for the area. The aim was to produce a pioneering low-energy building. The store is rooted to the site by earth banks, piled against the thick concrete side walls, which have a structural function – supporting the dramatic arched roof beams – but equally act as insulation. The roof itself is heavily insulated, with double glazing applied to the north light, which provides adequate illumination on all but the dullest days; artificial lighting is generally close to the shelving. Surplus heat and chill from the refrigerators is fed into 75-metre-deep boreholes for storage. Natural ventilation is supplied via an underfloor void, which carries all services. Vehicular servicing is from basement level, avoiding the untidy service areas that clutter most supermarkets.

The twin wind turbines that flank the entrances to the car park look like tokens, but the energy savings provided by the overall environmental package are significant: up to half on the typical demands of a conventional store of this size. It is easy to belittle the project as itself a token gesture, given the nature of the supermarket business, but it at least marks a step forward. Chetwood Associates' architecture is slick and of the moment, with none of the conviction of a Grimshaw but perhaps a closer understanding – from a firm with plenty of retail experience – of what shoppers like. The RIBA jury that gave it an award in 2000 considered it "an excellent building – full stop".

Above
Earth banks root the store to its exposed site and provide insulation to reinforce the progressive energy strategy of the scheme.

Opposite
The shaded glass façade and roof lights provide plenty of natural light – artificial lighting is used far more sparingly than in a typical supermarket.

FURTHER READING

Allinson, Ken, and Thornton, Victoria, *London's Contemporary Architecture: A Visitor's Guide*, 2nd edn,
    London (Architectural Press) 2000
Anderson, Robert, *The Great Court and the British Museum*, London (British Museum Press) 2000
Casson, Hugh, *New Sights of London*, London (London Transport) 1938
Chapman, Tony, *Architecture 04: The Guide to the RIBA Awards*, London (Merrell) 2004
Davies, Colin, *Hopkins 2*, London (Phaidon) 2001
Foster and Partners, *Foster Catalogue 2001*, Munich (Prestel) 2001
Future Systems, *Unique Building: Lord's Media Centre*, Chichester (Wiley-Academy) 2001
Hardingham, Samantha, *London: A Guide to Recent Architecture*, 5th edn, London (Ellipsis) 2001
Jackson, Alan A., *London's Termini*, Newton Abbot (David & Charles) 1969
Jencks, Charles, *Post Modern Triumphs in London*, Architectural Design Profile 91, London
    (Architectural Design) 1991
Jones, Edward, and Woodward, Christopher, *A Guide to the Architecture of London*, 3rd edn, London
    (Seven Dials) 2000
Lawrence, David, *Underground Architecture*, Harrow (Capital Transport) 1994
Lambot, Ian (ed.), *Reinventing the Wheel: The Construction of British Airways London Eye*, Haslemere
    (Watermark Publications) 2000
McKean, John, *Royal Festival Hall*, Buildings in Detail, London (Phaidon) 1992
Moore, Rowan, *et al.*, Building Tate Modern, London (Tate Gallery Publishing) 2000
Nairn, Ian, *Modern Buildings in London*, London (London Transport) 1964
Nairn, Ian, *Nairn's London*, Harmondsworth (Penguin) 1966
Powell, Kenneth, *City Reborn: Architecture and Regeneration in London, from Bankside to Dulwich*,
    London (Merrell) 2004
Powell, Kenneth, *Culture of Building: The Architecture of John McAslan + Partners*, London (Merrell) 2004
Powell, Kenneth, *The Jubilee Line Extension*, London (Laurence King) 2000
Powell, Kenneth, *et al.*, The National Portrait Gallery: An Architectural History, London
    (National Portrait Gallery) 2000
Powell, Kenneth, *New Architecture in Britain*, London (Merrell) 2003
Powell, Kenneth, *Richard Rogers: Complete Works, II*, London (Phaidon) 2001
Powell, Kenneth, *World Cities: London*, London (Academy Editions) 1992
Power, Mark, *Superstructure* [a photographic study of the building of the Millennium Dome], London
    (HarperCollins) 2000
Rogers, Richard (with Mark Fisher), *A New London*, London (Penguin) 1992
Rogers, Richard, *Cities for a Small Planet*, London (Faber & Faber) 1997
Sabbagh, Karl, *Power into Art: The Making of Tate Modern*, London (Penguin) 2001
Sudjic, Deyan, 'The Millennium Experience, London: A Dome, yet Different', in Rowan Moore (ed.),
    Vertigo: The Strange New World of the Contemporary City, London (Laurence King) 1999
Summerson, John, *Georgian London*, London (Pleiades Books) 1945 (and many subsequent editions)
Towards an Urban Renaissance: Final Report of the Urban Task Force, London (E & F.N. Spon) 1999
Unbuilt London, special issue of *The Architectural Review*, January 1988
Wilhide, Elizabeth, *The Millennium Dome*, London (HarperCollins) 1999
Wilkinson, Chris, and Eyre, James, *Bridging Art and Science: Wilkinson Eyre Architecture*, London
    (Booth-Clibborn Editions) 2001

PICTURE CREDITS